LES SECRETS DES ÉCONOMIES AU QUOTIDIEN

Sylvain MILON

SOMMAIRE

1. Introduction aux économies quotidiennes

2. Réduire les dépenses alimentaires

3. Économiser sur les factures d'énergie

4. Astuces pour économiser lors des achats en ligne

5. Réduire les dépenses liées au transport

6. Économiser sur les sorties et les loisirs

7. Gérer efficacement son budget

8. Économiser sur les produits de beauté et d'hygiène

9. Faire des économies en voyageant

10. Économiser sur les vêtements et la mode

11. Réduire les dépenses liées à la santé et aux soins médicaux

12. Économiser sur l'entretien de la maison

13. Astuces pour économiser sur les cadeaux et les occasions spéciales

14. Économiser pour l'avenir : conseils en matière d'épargne et d'investissement

15. Conclusion : adopter une mentalité d'économie au quotidien

INTRODUCTION

Les Secrets des Économies Quotidiennes est un guide pratique qui vous aidera à maîtriser l'art de faire des économies dans votre vie de tous les jours. Que vous cherchiez à épargner de l'argent, à rembourser des dettes ou à améliorer votre situation financière, ce livre vous fournira les outils nécessaires pour réaliser des économies significatives sans sacrifier votre qualité de vie.

Dans notre société actuelle, où les dépenses semblent augmenter sans cesse, il est essentiel de savoir comment gérer efficacement son argent. Cependant, beaucoup de gens se sentent dépassés et ne savent pas par où commencer. Les Secrets des Économies Quotidiennes vous offre un plan d'action étape par étape, avec des conseils pratiques et faciles à mettre en œuvre.

Le livre est divisé en quinze chapitres, chacun abordant un aspect spécifique des économies quotidiennes. Du budget alimentaire aux factures d'énergie, des achats en ligne aux sorties et aux loisirs, vous découvrirez une multitude d'astuces et de stratégies pour réduire vos dépenses et économiser de l'argent.

Chaque chapitre est conçu pour vous donner des conseils concrets et des exemples pratiques, vous permettant d'appliquer immédiatement les principes d'économie dans votre vie quotidienne. Que vous soyez un étudiant cherchant à économiser sur votre budget de collation ou un parent de famille nombreuse essayant de réduire les dépenses mensuelles, ce livre s'adresse à vous.

Ne laissez pas l'argent contrôler votre vie. Prenez le contrôle de vos finances et apprenez à faire des économies au quotidien. Les Secrets des Économies Quotidiennes vous accompagnera dans votre parcours vers une vie plus économe, tout en vous offrant la liberté et la tranquillité d'esprit financière que vous méritez.

CHAPITRE 1 : INTRODUCTION AUX ÉCONOMIES QUOTIDIENNES

Dans ce premier chapitre, nous allons explorer l'importance des économies quotidiennes et comprendre pourquoi il est essentiel de maîtriser cet aspect de nos vies financières. Nous découvrirons également les bénéfices que les économies peuvent apporter à long terme et comment adopter une mentalité d'économie au quotidien.

La société dans laquelle nous vivons est régie par la consommation et les dépenses excessives. Nous sommes constamment bombardés par des publicités nous incitant à acheter de nouveaux produits, à essayer de nouvelles expériences et à dépenser notre argent sans réfléchir. Cette mentalité de consommation frénétique peut nous amener à vivre au-dessus de nos moyens et à accumuler des dettes.

C'est pourquoi il est crucial de comprendre l'importance des économies quotidiennes. Faire des économies ne signifie pas se priver de tout plaisir ou vivre de manière austère. Au contraire, cela implique d'être conscient de ses dépenses, de prendre des décisions éclairées et de dépenser son argent de manière intelligente.

Les économies quotidiennes offrent de nombreux avantages à long terme. Premièrement, cela nous permet d'accumuler un fonds d'urgence. Avoir une réserve d'argent pour faire face aux imprévus tels que des réparations de voiture, des frais médicaux ou une perte d'emploi nous procure une tranquillité d'esprit précieuse. De plus, les économies peuvent nous aider à réaliser nos projets à long terme, tels que l'achat d'une maison, la création d'une entreprise ou la planification de notre retraite.

En adoptant une mentalité d'économie au quotidien, nous apprenons également à valoriser davantage notre argent. Au lieu de dépenser impulsivement, nous prenons le temps d'évaluer nos besoins réels et de trouver des moyens d'économiser. Cela nous permet de dépenser notre argent de manière plus réfléchie et de donner plus de valeur à nos achats.

Pour commencer à faire des économies au quotidien, il est essentiel de prendre conscience de nos habitudes de dépenses. Tenez un journal des dépenses pendant une semaine ou un mois pour avoir une vue d'ensemble de vos dépenses. Cela vous aidera à identifier les domaines où vous dépensez le plus et où vous pourriez réduire vos dépenses.

Une fois que vous avez identifié vos habitudes de dépenses, vous pouvez commencer à mettre en place des stratégies d'économie. Par exemple, vous pouvez établir un budget mensuel et allouer une certaine somme d'argent à chaque catégorie de dépenses. Cela vous permettra de mieux contrôler vos dépenses et d'identifier les domaines où vous pouvez réduire vos dépenses.

Une autre stratégie efficace est de rechercher des moyens d'économiser sur vos dépenses courantes. Par exemple, vous pouvez comparer les prix avant d'acheter, utiliser des coupons de réduction ou profiter des offres promotionnelles. De plus, vous pouvez envisager des alternatives moins coûteuses pour certaines dépenses, comme préparer vos repas à la maison au lieu de manger au restaurant.

Enfin, il est important de garder à l'esprit que les économies quotidiennes ne se limitent pas aux dépenses. Vous pouvez également économiser en adoptant des habitudes de vie économes, telles que la réduction de la consommation d'énergie, l'utilisation de transports en commun ou le recyclage. Ces petites actions peuvent avoir un impact significatif sur votre budget et sur l'environnement.

En conclusion, les économies quotidiennes jouent un rôle essentiel dans notre vie financière. Elles nous permettent de vivre de manière plus responsable, de construire un avenir financier solide et de donner plus de valeur à notre argent. En adoptant une mentalité d'économie au quotidien, vous serez en mesure de prendre le contrôle de vos finances et d'atteindre vos objectifs financiers à long terme.

CHAPITRE 2 : RÉDUIRE LES DÉPENSES ALIMENTAIRES

La nourriture est une dépense inévitable dans notre vie quotidienne, mais elle peut représenter une part importante de notre budget. Dans ce chapitre, nous allons explorer différentes stratégies pour réduire nos dépenses alimentaires sans compromettre la qualité de notre alimentation.

1. Planifier les repas : La planification des repas est une étape essentielle pour réduire les dépenses alimentaires. En planifiant à l'avance les repas de la semaine, vous pouvez établir une liste d'achats précise et éviter les achats impulsifs. Cela permet également d'éviter le gaspillage alimentaire, car vous achetez uniquement ce dont vous avez besoin.

2. Faire une liste de courses : Avant de vous rendre au supermarché, prenez le temps d'établir une liste de courses en vous basant sur vos repas planifiés. Cela vous évitera d'acheter des produits superflus et vous aidera à rester concentré sur les articles essentiels. Essayez de vous en tenir à votre liste autant que possible pour éviter les achats impulsifs.

3. Comparer les prix : Ne vous contentez pas d'acheter vos produits alimentaires dans un seul magasin. Prenez le temps de comparer les prix dans différentes enseignes, en ligne ou en magasin physique. Vous pourriez être surpris de constater à quel point les prix peuvent varier d'un endroit à l'autre. Optez pour les promotions et les réductions pour économiser davantage.

4. Privilégier les produits de saison : Les produits de saison sont souvent moins chers et plus frais. Ils sont également plus susceptibles d'être cultivés localement, ce qui réduit l'empreinte carbone liée à leur transport. Informez-vous sur les fruits, légumes et produits saisonniers de votre région et intégrez-les dans vos repas pour économiser tout en soutenant les producteurs locaux.

5. Cuisiner à la maison : Manger au restaurant ou acheter des plats préparés peut coûter cher à long terme. Privilégiez la cuisine faite maison, où vous avez le contrôle sur les ingrédients utilisés et les portions. Cuisiner à la maison permet également de préparer des repas en grandes quantités, que vous pouvez congeler et consommer ultérieurement, ce qui vous fera économiser du temps et de l'argent.

6. Éviter le gaspillage alimentaire : Le gaspillage alimentaire est non seulement une perte d'argent, mais aussi une source de préjudice pour l'environnement. Apprenez à gérer vos restes de manière créative en les intégrant dans de nouveaux plats. Utilisez des techniques de conservation, comme la mise en conserve ou la congélation, pour prolonger la durée de vie de vos aliments. De plus, soyez conscient des dates de péremption et utilisez les aliments avant qu'ils ne se gâtent.

7. Acheter en vrac : Lorsque cela est possible, optez pour l'achat

en vrac. Cela vous permet d'acheter la quantité exacte dont vous avez besoin, réduisant ainsi le gaspillage et les coûts associés aux emballages. Apportez vos propres contenants réutilisables pour remplir vos produits en vrac, tels que les céréales, les légumineuses et les épices.

8. Cultiver un jardin : Si vous disposez d'un espace extérieur, envisagez de cultiver votre propre jardin. Cultiver vos propres fruits, légumes et herbes vous permettra de réduire considérablement vos dépenses alimentaires. De plus, c'est une activité gratifiante qui vous connecte à la nature et vous permet de consommer des produits frais et de qualité.

En appliquant ces stratégies, vous pouvez réduire significativement vos dépenses alimentaires tout en préservant la qualité de votre alimentation. Réfléchissez à vos habitudes alimentaires et adoptez des changements progressifs pour construire une approche plus économique et durable en matière de nourriture. Votre porte-monnaie et votre santé vous en seront reconnaissants.

CHAPITRE 3 : ÉCONOMISER SUR LES FACTURES D'ÉNERGIE

Les factures d'énergie peuvent représenter une part importante de nos dépenses mensuelles. Dans ce chapitre, nous allons explorer différentes stratégies pour réduire nos dépenses énergétiques et économiser sur nos factures.

1. Isolation de la maison : L'isolation de la maison est essentielle pour réduire la consommation d'énergie. Assurez-vous que votre maison est correctement isolée en vérifiant les fenêtres, les portes, les murs et les combles. Des fenêtres bien étanches et des portes isolantes peuvent réduire les pertes de chaleur en hiver et préserver la fraîcheur en été, réduisant ainsi la nécessité de chauffer ou de climatiser excessivement.

2. Utilisation efficace du chauffage et de la climatisation : Réglez votre thermostat à une température confortable mais économique. En baissant le chauffage d'un degré ou en augmentant la climatisation d'un degré, vous pouvez réaliser des économies significatives sur votre consommation d'énergie. De plus, pensez à utiliser des thermostats programmables qui vous permettent de régler automatiquement la température en fonction de votre emploi du temps.

3. Éclairage économe en énergie : Remplacez les ampoules traditionnelles par des ampoules LED plus économes en énergie. Les ampoules LED consomment jusqu'à 80% moins d'énergie que les ampoules incandescentes et durent beaucoup plus longtemps. Éteignez également les lumières lorsque vous quittez une pièce et utilisez la lumière naturelle autant que possible pendant la journée.

4. Utilisation efficace des appareils électroménagers : Les appareils électroménagers peuvent représenter une part importante de la consommation d'énergie dans un foyer. Choisissez des appareils économes en énergie en optant pour des modèles certifiés Energy Star. Utilisez-les de manière efficace en évitant de les laisser en veille et en les débranchant lorsque vous ne les utilisez pas. Utilisez également des cycles de lavage à basse température pour la lessive et préférez le séchage à l'air libre plutôt que l'utilisation d'un sèche-linge.

5. Réduction de la consommation d'eau chaude : L'eau chaude peut représenter une part importante de vos factures d'énergie. Réduisez la température de votre chauffe-eau à 50-55 degrés Celsius et utilisez des douchettes et des robinets à débit réduit pour économiser l'eau chaude. Réparez également les fuites d'eau, car même une petite fuite peut entraîner une grande perte d'eau chaude et une augmentation de vos factures.

6. Utilisation efficace des appareils électroniques : Les appareils électroniques peuvent consommer de l'énergie même en mode veille. Utilisez des multiprises avec interrupteur pour éteindre complètement vos appareils électroniques lorsque vous ne les utilisez pas. Évitez également de laisser vos appareils en charge une fois qu'ils sont complètement chargés.

7. Utilisation responsable de l'eau et de l'électricité : Adoptez des habitudes responsables en matière d'utilisation de l'eau et de l'électricité. Prenez des douches plus courtes, utilisez des lave-vaisselle et des machines à laver pleins, et éteignez les lumières et les appareils lorsque vous ne les utilisez pas. Ces petits gestes peuvent avoir un impact significatif sur vos factures d'énergie.

En mettant en pratique ces stratégies, vous pouvez réduire vos dépenses énergétiques et économiser sur vos factures. En plus des avantages financiers, vous contribuerez également à la préservation de l'environnement en réduisant votre empreinte écologique. Adoptez ces habitudes d'économie d'énergie dans votre vie quotidienne et vous constaterez une différence positive à la fois sur vos factures et sur l'environnement.

CHAPITRE 4 : ASTUCES POUR ÉCONOMISER LORS DES ACHATS EN LIGNE

Les achats en ligne sont devenus une pratique courante dans notre société connectée. Cependant, cela ne signifie pas que nous devons dépenser une fortune pour obtenir ce dont nous avons besoin. Dans ce chapitre, nous allons explorer différentes astuces pour économiser lors des achats en ligne et maximiser notre pouvoir d'achat.

1. Comparer les prix : L'un des avantages majeurs des achats en ligne est la possibilité de comparer facilement les prix entre différents vendeurs. Avant d'effectuer un achat, prenez le temps de rechercher le même produit sur différents sites web et comparez les prix. Assurez-vous également de prendre en compte les frais de livraison et les éventuels codes de réduction disponibles.

2. Utiliser des codes de réduction : Avant de finaliser votre achat, recherchez des codes de réduction. De nombreux sites web proposent des codes promotionnels et des coupons que vous pouvez utiliser pour obtenir des remises sur vos achats en ligne.

Il existe également des extensions de navigateur qui peuvent automatiquement rechercher et appliquer les codes de réduction disponibles lors de votre processus d'achat.

3. Profiter des promotions et des soldes : Les achats en ligne offrent souvent des promotions spéciales et des soldes. Gardez un œil sur les sites web de vos boutiques préférées pour connaître les offres en cours. Certaines périodes de l'année, comme le Black Friday, le Cyber Monday ou les soldes d'été, sont particulièrement propices pour réaliser des économies importantes.

4. Abonnement aux newsletters : Inscrivez-vous aux newsletters des sites de commerce en ligne. De nombreux détaillants envoient des offres exclusives et des codes de réduction aux abonnés de leur liste de diffusion. Cela vous permettra d'être informé des promotions et des nouveautés, et de ne pas manquer les offres spéciales.

5. Utiliser des sites de cashback : Les sites de cashback vous permettent de récupérer une partie de l'argent dépensé lors de vos achats en ligne. Inscrivez-vous sur ces plateformes et passez par leurs liens d'affiliation pour effectuer vos achats. Vous accumulerez ainsi des remboursements qui pourront être transférés sur votre compte bancaire ou utilisés pour de futurs achats.

6. Attendre les périodes de soldes : Si vous n'avez pas besoin d'un article immédiatement, envisagez d'attendre les périodes de soldes pour effectuer votre achat. Les détaillants en ligne proposent souvent des réductions importantes lors des soldes saisonnières, ce qui peut vous permettre d'économiser considérablement sur vos achats.

7. Lire les avis et les commentaires : Avant d'acheter un produit en ligne, prenez le temps de lire les avis et les commentaires des autres utilisateurs. Cela vous aidera à évaluer la qualité du produit et à prendre une décision éclairée. Méfiez-vous également des offres trop alléchantes ou des sites web douteux. Il est important de faire preuve de prudence et de vérifier la réputation du vendeur avant de faire un achat.

8. Éviter les achats impulsifs : Les achats en ligne peuvent être tentants, mais il est important de résister aux achats impulsifs. Prenez le temps de réfléchir à vos besoins réels et à l'utilité du produit avant de l'ajouter à votre panier. Établissez une liste de souhaits et attendez quelques jours avant de finaliser votre achat. Cela vous permettra de prendre du recul et d'éviter les dépenses inutiles.

En mettant en pratique ces astuces, vous pouvez économiser considérablement lors de vos achats en ligne. N'oubliez pas d'être vigilant, de comparer les prix, de rechercher des codes de réduction et de profiter des promotions spéciales. Les achats en ligne peuvent être une opportunité de réaliser de bonnes affaires, à condition de faire preuve de prudence et de stratégie lors de vos transactions en ligne.

CHAPITRE 5 : RÉDUIRE LES DÉPENSES LIÉES AU TRANSPORT

Le transport est une dépense incontournable dans nos vies, que ce soit pour se rendre au travail, faire ses courses ou voyager. Cependant, il est possible de réduire ces dépenses en adoptant des habitudes et des choix plus économiques. Dans ce chapitre, nous allons explorer différentes stratégies pour réduire les dépenses liées au transport et économiser de l'argent.

1. Utiliser les transports en commun : Les transports en commun, tels que les bus, les métros et les trains, sont souvent moins chers que les véhicules personnels. Optez pour les transports en commun lorsque cela est possible, surtout si vous vivez dans une zone bien desservie. Les abonnements mensuels ou annuels peuvent également offrir des réductions supplémentaires.

2. Partager les trajets : Si vous devez vous rendre au travail ou à d'autres destinations régulièrement, envisagez le covoiturage. Partager les trajets avec des collègues ou des amis permet de diviser les coûts du carburant et des péages. Vous pouvez également vous renseigner sur les plateformes de covoiturage qui mettent en relation des conducteurs et des passagers partageant le même itinéraire.

3. Opter pour le vélo ou la marche : Pour les trajets courts, privilégiez le vélo ou la marche. Non seulement vous économiserez sur les frais de carburant et de stationnement, mais vous améliorerez également votre santé en restant actif. Ces modes de transport écologiques et économiques sont également idéaux pour les déplacements en centre-ville où la circulation peut être dense.

4. Entretenir son véhicule : Si vous possédez une voiture, assurez-vous de bien l'entretenir pour minimiser les dépenses liées au carburant et aux réparations. Vérifiez régulièrement la pression des pneus, faites des vidanges d'huile régulières et assurez-vous que le moteur est en bon état. Un véhicule bien entretenu consomme moins de carburant et a une durée de vie plus longue.

5. Éviter les embouteillages : Les embouteillages peuvent augmenter considérablement la consommation de carburant et prolonger la durée de vos trajets. Planifiez vos déplacements en évitant les heures de pointe si possible, utilisez des applications de navigation pour trouver les itinéraires les plus rapides et envisagez des alternatives, comme le télétravail, pour réduire le nombre de trajets en voiture.

6. Comparer les prix des carburants : Les prix du carburant peuvent varier d'une station-service à l'autre. Avant de faire le plein, consultez les différentes stations-service de votre région pour trouver le carburant au meilleur prix. Utilisez également les applications mobiles ou les sites web qui vous indiquent les prix du carburant en temps réel.

7. Privilégier les véhicules économes en carburant : Si vous envisagez d'acheter un nouveau véhicule, renseignez-vous sur les modèles économes en carburant. Les véhicules hybrides,

électriques ou dotés de moteurs diesel plus efficaces peuvent vous permettre d'économiser sur les coûts du carburant à long terme.

8. Utiliser des services de partage de véhicules : Si vous avez besoin d'une voiture seulement de temps en temps, envisagez d'utiliser des services de partage de véhicules tels que la location de voiture à l'heure ou à la journée. Cela peut s'avérer plus économique que la possession d'un véhicule personnel, car vous ne payez que lorsque vous en avez réellement besoin.

En mettant en pratique ces stratégies, vous pouvez réduire considérablement vos dépenses liées au transport. Que ce soit en optant pour les transports en commun, en partageant les trajets ou en choisissant des modes de transport plus économiques, chaque petit changement peut avoir un impact significatif sur votre budget. Soyez conscient de vos options et faites des choix judicieux pour économiser de l'argent tout en vous déplaçant efficacement.

CHAPITRE 6 :
ÉCONOMISER SUR
LES SORTIES ET
LES LOISIRS

Les sorties et les loisirs sont des éléments importants de notre vie sociale, mais ils peuvent également peser lourdement sur notre budget. Dans ce chapitre, nous allons explorer différentes astuces pour économiser sur les sorties et les loisirs, tout en profitant de moments agréables et divertissants.

1. Rechercher des offres spéciales : Avant de planifier une sortie ou une activité de loisir, renseignez-vous sur les offres spéciales et les réductions disponibles. De nombreux sites web proposent des offres promotionnelles, des coupons ou des packages qui peuvent vous permettre d'économiser sur les billets d'entrée, les repas ou les activités. Prenez le temps de comparer les prix et de choisir l'option la plus avantageuse.

2. Profiter des tarifs réduits : De nombreux lieux de divertissement, tels que les musées, les cinémas ou les parcs d'attractions, offrent des tarifs réduits à certaines heures de la journée ou à certains groupes spécifiques (étudiants, personnes

âgées, familles, etc.). Renseignez-vous sur ces offres et planifiez vos sorties en conséquence pour bénéficier de tarifs plus avantageux.

3. Organiser des sorties gratuites ou à faible coût : Il existe de nombreuses activités de loisirs gratuites ou à faible coût. Organisez des sorties en plein air, des pique-niques, des randonnées ou des visites de lieux historiques ou culturels. Explorez les parcs locaux, assistez à des événements communautaires ou participez à des ateliers gratuits. Ces activités vous permettront de passer du temps de qualité sans dépenser beaucoup d'argent.

4. Privilégier les abonnements et les pass : Si vous avez l'intention de fréquenter régulièrement un lieu de divertissement, envisagez de souscrire un abonnement ou d'acheter un pass. De nombreux théâtres, clubs de sport, centres de loisirs et musées proposent des abonnements ou des pass mensuels ou annuels qui offrent des tarifs réduits ou l'accès illimité à certaines activités. Faites le calcul pour déterminer si ces options valent la peine en fonction de votre utilisation prévue.

5. Organiser des soirées à la maison : Les sorties peuvent être coûteuses, surtout lorsque vous ajoutez les dépenses liées aux repas et aux boissons. Organisez des soirées à la maison en invitant des amis ou des proches pour des jeux de société, des projections de films, des repas partagés ou des barbecues. Non seulement cela réduit les coûts, mais cela crée également un environnement convivial et intime.

6. Utiliser des applications et des sites web de réservation : De nombreuses applications et sites web de réservation offrent des tarifs réduits ou des offres spéciales sur les restaurants, les activités de loisirs, les spectacles et les événements. Utilisez ces

outils pour trouver les meilleures offres disponibles dans votre région et économiser sur vos sorties.

7. Pratiquer des loisirs abordables : Trouvez des loisirs abordables qui correspondent à vos intérêts. Optez pour des activités gratuites ou peu coûteuses telles que la lecture, le jardinage, le bricolage, le yoga à domicile ou la cuisine. Explorez également les ressources en ligne, comme les tutoriels ou les cours gratuits, pour découvrir de nouvelles activités sans avoir à dépenser beaucoup d'argent.

8. Établir un budget pour les sorties et les loisirs : Fixez-vous un budget mensuel pour les sorties et les loisirs et respectez-le. Cela vous permettra de contrôler vos dépenses et de prendre des décisions plus réfléchies. Vous pouvez également réserver une partie de votre budget pour des activités spéciales ou des événements que vous souhaitez particulièrement vivre.

En mettant en pratique ces astuces, vous pouvez profiter de sorties et de loisirs tout en maîtrisant vos dépenses. Recherchez les offres spéciales, privilégiez les activités gratuites ou à faible coût, organisez des sorties à la maison et établissez un budget pour garder le contrôle sur vos dépenses de loisirs. Rappelez-vous qu'il est possible de se divertir sans vider son portefeuille, il suffit d'être créatif et d'explorer toutes les options disponibles.

CHAPITRE 7 : GÉRER EFFICACEMENT SON BUDGET

La gestion efficace de son budget est essentielle pour atteindre ses objectifs financiers et assurer sa stabilité financière. Dans ce chapitre, nous allons explorer différentes stratégies pour gérer votre budget de manière efficace et optimiser vos dépenses.

1. Faire le point sur ses revenus et ses dépenses : La première étape de la gestion du budget consiste à avoir une vision claire de vos revenus et de vos dépenses. Prenez le temps d'évaluer vos revenus mensuels, y compris les salaires, les revenus complémentaires et les autres sources de revenus. Ensuite, examinez vos dépenses en détail, en catégorisant les dépenses fixes (loyer, factures, etc.) et les dépenses variables (alimentation, loisirs, etc.). Cette évaluation vous aidera à identifier où va votre argent et à prendre des décisions éclairées pour optimiser votre budget.

2. Établir un budget réaliste : Utilisez les informations recueillies pour établir un budget réaliste. Allouez une partie de vos revenus à chaque catégorie de dépenses, y compris l'épargne. Fixez des objectifs financiers clairs, tels que rembourser une dette, épargner pour un achat important ou constituer un fonds d'urgence, et incluez-les dans votre budget. Assurez-vous que vos dépenses ne

dépassent pas vos revenus et ajustez si nécessaire pour atteindre un équilibre financier.

3. Suivre ses dépenses : Tenez un suivi régulier de vos dépenses pour vous assurer de respecter votre budget. Vous pouvez le faire en utilisant des applications de suivi des dépenses, en enregistrant vos dépenses dans un journal ou en utilisant des feuilles de calcul. L'objectif est de savoir où va votre argent, de détecter les zones où vous pourriez réduire vos dépenses et de garder une trace de vos progrès vers vos objectifs financiers.

4. Prioriser l'épargne : L'épargne est un élément crucial de la gestion du budget. Fixez-vous un objectif d'épargne mensuel et incluez-le dans votre budget dès le départ. Faites en sorte que l'épargne soit une priorité, tout comme le paiement de vos autres factures. Automatisez vos épargnes en mettant en place des virements automatiques vers un compte d'épargne chaque mois. Cela vous aidera à constituer une réserve financière et à vous préparer aux imprévus.

5. Réduire les dépenses superflues : Analysez vos dépenses et identifiez les postes où vous pourriez réduire vos dépenses superflues. Cela peut inclure des abonnements non utilisés, des dépenses impulsives ou des habitudes de consommation excessives. Identifiez ces domaines et prenez des mesures pour les réduire ou les éliminer. Par exemple, vous pourriez résilier certains abonnements, adopter des alternatives moins coûteuses ou pratiquer une consommation plus consciente.

6. Négocier les factures et les contrats : Ne sous-estimez pas le pouvoir de la négociation. Contactez vos fournisseurs de services (internet, téléphone, assurance, etc.) pour évaluer si vous pouvez obtenir de meilleurs tarifs ou des offres promotionnelles. Explorez également les offres concurrentes et utilisez-les comme levier

pour négocier avec votre fournisseur actuel. La négociation peut vous permettre d'économiser considérablement sur vos factures mensuelles.

7. Prévoir les dépenses futures : Anticipez les dépenses futures telles que les frais d'entretien de voiture, les réparations à domicile ou les dépenses liées aux vacances. Prévoir ces dépenses dans votre budget vous permettra de mettre de l'argent de côté à l'avance et de ne pas être pris au dépourvu lorsque ces dépenses surviendront. Vous pouvez créer un fonds séparé pour ces dépenses à long terme.

8. Revoir régulièrement votre budget : La gestion du budget est un processus continu. Revenez régulièrement sur votre budget, évaluez vos progrès et apportez les ajustements nécessaires. Votre situation financière peut évoluer, de nouveaux objectifs peuvent émerger et certaines dépenses peuvent varier. Soyez flexible et adaptez votre budget en conséquence pour rester en contrôle de vos finances.

En mettant en pratique ces stratégies, vous serez en mesure de gérer efficacement votre budget et d'optimiser vos dépenses. La gestion du budget vous permet de contrôler vos finances, d'atteindre vos objectifs financiers et de vivre de manière plus sereine sur le plan financier. Soyez diligent, suivez votre budget et ajustez-le en fonction de vos besoins et de vos objectifs.

CHAPITRE 8 :
ÉCONOMISER SUR
LES PRODUITS DE
BEAUTÉ ET D'HYGIÈNE

Les produits de beauté et d'hygiène peuvent représenter une part importante de nos dépenses mensuelles. Cependant, il est possible de réduire ces dépenses en adoptant des stratégies intelligentes et économiques. Dans ce chapitre, nous allons explorer différentes astuces pour économiser sur les produits de beauté et d'hygiène tout en prenant soin de soi.

1. Faire une liste des produits nécessaires : Avant d'acheter des produits de beauté et d'hygiène, faites une liste des articles dont vous avez réellement besoin. Évitez les achats impulsifs et concentrez-vous sur les produits essentiels. En ayant une liste précise, vous éviterez d'acheter des produits superflus et vous pourrez mieux contrôler vos dépenses.

2. Comparer les prix : Ne vous contentez pas d'acheter vos produits dans un seul magasin. Prenez le temps de comparer les prix dans différents magasins physiques et en ligne. Vous pourriez trouver des différences significatives de prix pour les mêmes

produits. N'hésitez pas à profiter des offres promotionnelles et des réductions pour économiser davantage.

3. Opter pour les marques abordables : Les marques de produits de beauté et d'hygiène proposent souvent des alternatives abordables sans compromettre la qualité. Faites des recherches et identifiez les marques qui offrent des produits de qualité à des prix plus abordables. Vous pouvez également consulter les avis et les commentaires en ligne pour avoir une idée de la performance des produits avant de les acheter.

4. Privilégier les produits multi-usages : Choisissez des produits qui ont plusieurs usages. Par exemple, optez pour un nettoyant visage qui peut également servir de démaquillant ou pour un baume à lèvres qui peut être utilisé comme hydratant pour les cuticules. En utilisant des produits multi-usages, vous réduirez le nombre de produits à acheter et économiserez de l'argent.

5. Utiliser des échantillons et des formats voyage : Profitez des échantillons gratuits ou des formats voyage proposés par les marques. Cela vous permettra de tester les produits avant de les acheter en taille réelle. De plus, les formats voyage sont moins chers que les versions complètes et sont idéaux pour les déplacements ou pour une utilisation temporaire.

6. Faire soi-même certains produits : Vous pouvez économiser de l'argent en fabriquant vous-même certains produits de beauté et d'hygiène. Par exemple, vous pouvez créer votre propre gommage pour le corps en mélangeant du sucre et de l'huile d'olive, ou fabriquer un masque capillaire nourrissant à base d'ingrédients naturels. Il existe de nombreuses recettes et tutoriels en ligne pour vous guider dans la création de vos propres produits.

7. Utiliser les promotions et les soldes : Surveillez les promotions et les soldes pour profiter de réductions sur les produits de beauté et d'hygiène. Beaucoup de magasins et de sites web proposent des offres spéciales, telles que des "achetez-en un, obtenez-en un gratuitement" ou des remises importantes. Planifiez vos achats en conséquence pour tirer parti de ces offres avantageuses.

8. Étirer les produits jusqu'à la dernière goutte : Utilisez les produits jusqu'à leur épuisement complet. Par exemple, coupez les tubes de dentifrice pour en extraire chaque dernière portion ou diluez les restes de shampoing pour en faire un lavage final. En utilisant les produits jusqu'à la dernière goutte, vous maximiserez leur utilisation et prolongerez leur durée de vie, ce qui vous évitera d'avoir à en racheter fréquemment.

En mettant en pratique ces astuces, vous pouvez économiser sur vos dépenses liées aux produits de beauté et d'hygiène. Soyez conscient de vos besoins réels, comparez les prix, optez pour des marques abordables et profitez des promotions. N'hésitez pas à être créatif et à fabriquer certains produits vous-même. Avec ces stratégies, vous pourrez prendre soin de vous tout en respectant votre budget.

CHAPITRE 9 : FAIRE DES ÉCONOMIES EN VOYAGEANT

Le voyage peut être une expérience merveilleuse, mais cela ne signifie pas que vous devez dépenser une fortune pour explorer de nouveaux endroits. Dans ce chapitre, nous allons explorer différentes astuces pour faire des économies en voyageant et profiter de vacances abordables.

1. Planifier à l'avance : L'une des clés pour économiser en voyageant est de planifier à l'avance. Réservez vos billets d'avion et vos hébergements plusieurs mois à l'avance pour profiter des tarifs les plus bas. De plus, en planifiant à l'avance, vous avez le temps de rechercher les meilleures offres et de comparer les prix pour chaque aspect de votre voyage.

2. Voyager pendant la basse saison : Les tarifs des vols, des hôtels et des attractions touristiques peuvent varier considérablement en fonction de la saison. Voyager pendant la basse saison vous permet de bénéficier de tarifs réduits et d'éviter les foules de touristes. En plus de faire des économies, vous pourrez profiter d'une expérience de voyage plus authentique.

3. Utiliser des comparateurs de vols et d'hôtels : Utilisez des sites web et des applications de comparaison pour trouver les vols et les hébergements les moins chers. Ces outils vous permettent de comparer les prix de différentes compagnies aériennes et hôtels en un seul endroit, vous faisant économiser du temps et de l'argent. N'oubliez pas de consulter les avis et les commentaires des voyageurs pour vous assurer de la qualité des prestations.

4. Privilégier les logements économiques : Optez pour des hébergements économiques tels que les auberges de jeunesse, les chambres d'hôtes ou les locations de vacances. Ces options sont souvent moins chères que les grands hôtels, tout en offrant une expérience plus authentique et conviviale. Vous pouvez également envisager le couchsurfing, une pratique où les voyageurs sont hébergés gratuitement par des habitants.

5. Explorer les options de transport local : Au lieu de prendre des taxis ou de louer une voiture, explorez les options de transport local. Utilisez les transports en commun, comme les bus, les métros ou les trains, qui sont souvent beaucoup moins chers. Vous pouvez également opter pour la location de vélos ou marcher pour explorer les destinations locales, ce qui vous permettra également de découvrir la ville d'une manière plus immersive.

6. Manger dans des endroits locaux : Évitez les restaurants touristiques chers et privilégiez les endroits fréquentés par les habitants. Manger dans des restaurants locaux ou même acheter de la nourriture dans les marchés et les épiceries peut être beaucoup moins cher. Cela vous permettra également de découvrir la cuisine locale et d'interagir avec les habitants.

7. Profiter des activités gratuites ou à faible coût : Renseignez-vous sur les activités gratuites ou à faible coût disponibles dans

votre destination. De nombreuses villes offrent des visites guidées gratuites, des musées gratuits certains jours de la semaine ou des événements culturels ou artistiques accessibles à tous. Consultez les agendas locaux et faites des recherches en ligne pour trouver des options économiques pour vous divertir.

8. Limiter les souvenirs coûteux : Les souvenirs peuvent rapidement devenir une dépense importante pendant un voyage. Limitez les achats impulsifs de souvenirs coûteux et privilégiez des souvenirs plus abordables tels que des cartes postales, des magnets ou des objets artisanaux locaux. Vous pouvez également choisir de prendre des photos pour immortaliser vos expériences sans dépenser d'argent.

En mettant en pratique ces astuces, vous pouvez faire des économies significatives en voyageant. Planifiez à l'avance, comparez les prix, voyagez pendant la basse saison et utilisez des hébergements et des transports économiques. Explorez les options locales, profitez des activités gratuites et limitez les dépenses excessives. Rappelez-vous que le voyage n'est pas seulement une question de destination, mais aussi de l'expérience que vous en faites.

CHAPITRE 10 : ÉCONOMISER SUR LES VÊTEMENTS ET LA MODE

La mode peut être une passion pour certains, mais cela ne signifie pas que vous devez dépenser une fortune pour rester à la pointe des tendances. Dans ce chapitre, nous allons explorer différentes astuces pour économiser sur les vêtements et la mode tout en restant stylé.

1. Faire un inventaire de sa garde-robe : Avant de faire des achats, faites un inventaire de votre garde-robe. Identifiez les pièces que vous possédez déjà et évaluez leur état et leur polyvalence. Cela vous aidera à mieux comprendre ce dont vous avez vraiment besoin et à éviter d'acheter des articles similaires ou inutiles.

2. Privilégier la qualité plutôt que la quantité : Optez pour des vêtements de qualité plutôt que des articles bon marché qui s'usent rapidement. Même si cela signifie dépenser un peu plus à l'achat, les vêtements de qualité dureront plus longtemps et vous feront économiser de l'argent à long terme. Recherchez des marques réputées pour leur durabilité et leur qualité de

fabrication.

3. Profiter des soldes et des promotions : Surveillez les soldes et les promotions pour obtenir des vêtements à prix réduits. Les magasins proposent souvent des réductions importantes lors des périodes de soldes saisonnières. Vous pouvez également vous inscrire aux newsletters des marques pour être informé des offres spéciales et des codes de réduction.

4. Acheter d'occasion : Les vêtements d'occasion sont une excellente façon d'économiser sur les dépenses de mode. Explorez les friperies, les magasins de seconde main ou les sites web de vente de vêtements d'occasion. Vous pouvez trouver des pièces uniques et de qualité à des prix considérablement réduits. Veillez à inspecter attentivement les vêtements pour vous assurer de leur bon état.

5. Échanger ou emprunter des vêtements : Organisez des échanges de vêtements avec vos amis, votre famille ou même vos collègues. Vous pouvez également envisager d'emprunter des vêtements pour des occasions spéciales plutôt que d'acheter de nouvelles tenues. Cela vous permettra de diversifier votre garde-robe sans dépenser d'argent supplémentaire.

6. Apprendre à faire des retouches : Si vous possédez des compétences de base en couture, vous pouvez économiser de l'argent en faisant vos propres retouches. Apprenez à raccourcir des pantalons, à ajuster des robes ou à remplacer des boutons. Vous pourrez ainsi donner une nouvelle vie à vos vêtements existants au lieu d'en acheter de nouveaux.

7. Privilégier les basiques intemporels : Investissez dans des basiques intemporels tels que des jeans de qualité, des chemises

blanches, des blazers noirs, etc. Ces pièces polyvalentes peuvent être facilement combinées avec d'autres éléments de votre garde-robe, ce qui vous permet de créer différents looks sans avoir à acheter de nouvelles tenues à chaque fois.

8. Suivre les tendances avec parcimonie : Ne cédez pas à toutes les tendances éphémères. Choisissez judicieusement les tendances auxquelles vous souhaitez vous adhérer et n'achetez que quelques pièces clés pour compléter votre garde-robe. Cela vous évitera de dépenser de l'argent pour des articles qui deviendront rapidement obsolètes.

9. Prendre soin de ses vêtements : Prenez bien soin de vos vêtements pour prolonger leur durée de vie. Respectez les instructions de lavage, rangez-les correctement et réparez-les dès que nécessaire. Plus vous prenez soin de vos vêtements, moins vous aurez à en racheter fréquemment.

En mettant en pratique ces astuces, vous pouvez économiser sur les vêtements et la mode tout en restant à la pointe des tendances. Faites un inventaire de votre garde-robe, privilégiez la qualité, profitez des soldes, explorez les vêtements d'occasion et apprenez à faire des retouches. N'oubliez pas de choisir des basiques intemporels et de prendre soin de vos vêtements pour les faire durer plus longtemps.

CHAPITRE 11 : RÉDUIRE LES DÉPENSES LIÉES À LA SANTÉ ET AUX SOINS MÉDICAUX

La santé est une priorité, mais cela ne signifie pas que vous devez dépenser une fortune pour vous maintenir en bonne forme et accéder à des soins médicaux de qualité. Dans ce chapitre, nous allons explorer différentes astuces pour réduire les dépenses liées à la santé et aux soins médicaux tout en préservant votre bien-être.

1. Prévenir les problèmes de santé : Adoptez un mode de vie sain pour prévenir les problèmes de santé et réduire les dépenses médicales à long terme. Maintenez une alimentation équilibrée, faites de l'exercice régulièrement, évitez le tabac et limitez votre consommation d'alcool. En prenant soin de votre santé, vous pouvez éviter de nombreux problèmes de santé coûteux.

2. Faire des examens de santé réguliers : La prévention est essentielle pour détecter les problèmes de santé à un stade

précoce. Faites des examens de santé réguliers, tels que des bilans sanguins, des examens dentaires et des dépistages, pour identifier tout problème de santé potentiel. En détectant les problèmes de santé à un stade précoce, vous pouvez éviter des complications coûteuses à long terme.

3. Comparer les tarifs des professionnels de santé : Lorsque vous devez consulter un professionnel de santé, prenez le temps de comparer les tarifs. Les prix peuvent varier d'un professionnel à l'autre, même pour les mêmes services médicaux. Recherchez des avis et des recommandations, puis comparez les tarifs pour trouver un professionnel de santé abordable et de qualité.

4. Utiliser les services de santé gratuits ou à faible coût : Renseignez-vous sur les services de santé gratuits ou à faible coût disponibles dans votre région. De nombreux gouvernements offrent des programmes de santé publique qui fournissent des services médicaux à des tarifs réduits ou gratuits. Vous pouvez également explorer les cliniques communautaires, les centres de santé locaux ou les programmes d'assistance médicale pour trouver des soins médicaux abordables.

5. Souscrire à une assurance santé adaptée : Si vous ne disposez pas déjà d'une assurance santé, explorez les différentes options disponibles et choisissez une assurance adaptée à vos besoins. Comparez les polices d'assurance pour trouver une couverture abordable qui correspond à vos besoins médicaux. Assurez-vous de comprendre les conditions, les limites et les exclusions de votre assurance pour éviter les surprises financières.

6. Utiliser les médicaments génériques : Lorsque vous avez besoin de médicaments, demandez à votre médecin ou à votre pharmacien s'il existe des versions génériques disponibles. Les médicaments génériques sont des alternatives moins coûteuses

aux médicaments de marque, mais ils contiennent les mêmes principes actifs et sont tout aussi efficaces. En choisissant des médicaments génériques, vous pouvez réaliser des économies significatives sur vos dépenses de médicaments.

7. Faire une recherche sur les coûts des médicaments : Avant d'acheter des médicaments, faites une recherche sur les différents fournisseurs et comparez les prix. Vous pouvez trouver des variations de prix importantes d'une pharmacie à l'autre. N'hésitez pas à demander des renseignements sur les options les plus abordables auprès de votre médecin ou de votre pharmacien.

8. Se renseigner sur les programmes d'aide financière : Certains médicaments coûteux ou traitements spécifiques peuvent bénéficier de programmes d'aide financière. Renseignez-vous auprès des fabricants de médicaments ou des organismes de santé pour savoir si vous êtes éligible à des programmes de réduction de coûts ou d'aide financière.

En mettant en pratique ces astuces, vous pouvez réduire vos dépenses liées à la santé et aux soins médicaux tout en préservant votre bien-être. Prévenez les problèmes de santé, faites des examens réguliers, comparez les tarifs des professionnels de santé et utilisez les services de santé gratuits ou à faible coût. Souscrivez à une assurance santé adaptée, privilégiez les médicaments génériques, faites des recherches sur les coûts des médicaments et renseignez-vous sur les programmes d'aide financière. La gestion responsable de votre santé peut vous aider à économiser de l'argent et à vous assurer un avenir sain.

CHAPITRE 12 : ÉCONOMISER SUR L'ENTRETIEN DE LA MAISON

L'entretien de la maison est une tâche incontournable, mais cela ne signifie pas que vous devez dépenser une fortune pour maintenir votre maison en bon état. Dans ce chapitre, nous allons explorer différentes astuces pour économiser sur l'entretien de la maison et réduire vos dépenses.

1. Planifier les tâches d'entretien : Faites un calendrier des tâches d'entretien de votre maison et planifiez-les à l'avance. Cela vous permettra de vous organiser, de ne pas oublier les tâches importantes et de prévenir les problèmes potentiels. L'entretien régulier vous aidera à éviter des réparations coûteuses à long terme.

2. Faire les réparations soi-même : Apprenez à effectuer vous-même certaines réparations et petits travaux dans votre maison. De nombreuses ressources en ligne proposent des tutoriels et des guides pour vous guider dans les réparations courantes. En faisant les réparations vous-même, vous économiserez sur les coûts de

main-d'œuvre.

3. Utiliser des produits d'entretien faits maison : Évitez d'acheter des produits d'entretien coûteux en optant pour des alternatives faites maison. Par exemple, vous pouvez utiliser du vinaigre blanc et du bicarbonate de soude pour nettoyer les surfaces, du citron pour enlever les taches et du savon de Marseille pour la lessive. Ces produits sont économiques, écologiques et tout aussi efficaces.

4. Économiser sur l'énergie : Réduisez vos dépenses d'énergie en adoptant des habitudes économes. Éteignez les lumières lorsque vous quittez une pièce, utilisez des ampoules à économie d'énergie, programmez votre thermostat pour réguler la température et débranchez les appareils électroniques lorsqu'ils ne sont pas utilisés. Ces petites actions peuvent réduire considérablement vos factures d'énergie.

5. Entretenir régulièrement les appareils ménagers : Faites l'entretien régulier de vos appareils ménagers pour prolonger leur durée de vie et éviter des réparations coûteuses. Nettoyez les filtres de la hotte de cuisine, dégivrez régulièrement votre réfrigérateur, nettoyez les conduits d'aération du sèche-linge et faites une maintenance régulière des systèmes de climatisation et de chauffage.

6. Réutiliser et recycler : Donnez une seconde vie aux objets plutôt que de les jeter. Réutilisez les bocaux en verre pour le stockage, transformez les vieux vêtements en chiffons de nettoyage et recyclez les matériaux tels que le carton, le verre et le plastique. En recyclant et en réutilisant, vous réduirez les dépenses d'achat de nouveaux produits.

7. Acheter des fournitures en vrac : Économisez sur les produits

d'entretien en achetant des fournitures en vrac. Achetez des produits en grande quantité, tels que le papier toilette, les produits de nettoyage ou les sacs poubelle, pour obtenir des prix réduits par unité. Assurez-vous de stocker correctement ces fournitures pour qu'elles restent en bon état jusqu'à leur utilisation.

8. Faire appel à des professionnels locaux : Lorsque vous avez besoin de services d'entretien professionnels, privilégiez les entreprises locales. Non seulement cela soutient l'économie locale, mais cela peut également vous permettre de bénéficier de tarifs compétitifs. Demandez des recommandations et comparez les prix pour trouver des professionnels fiables et abordables.

En mettant en pratique ces astuces, vous pouvez économiser sur l'entretien de votre maison tout en préservant sa qualité et sa valeur. Planifiez les tâches d'entretien, effectuez certaines réparations vous-même, utilisez des produits d'entretien faits maison et adoptez des habitudes économes en énergie. Entretenez régulièrement vos appareils ménagers, réutilisez et recyclez, achetez des fournitures en vrac et faites appel à des professionnels locaux lorsque nécessaire. En prenant soin de votre maison de manière économique, vous économiserez de l'argent à long terme tout en maintenant un environnement propre et confortable.

CHAPITRE 13 : ASTUCES POUR ÉCONOMISER SUR LES CADEAUX ET LES OCCASIONS SPÉCIALES

Les cadeaux et les occasions spéciales peuvent être des moments joyeux, mais cela ne signifie pas que vous devez dépenser une fortune pour montrer votre affection et célébrer avec vos proches. Dans ce chapitre, nous allons explorer différentes astuces pour économiser sur les cadeaux et les occasions spéciales tout en préservant leur signification et leur valeur.

1. Établir un budget : Avant de faire des achats pour des cadeaux ou des occasions spéciales, établissez un budget clair. Déterminez combien vous êtes prêt à dépenser pour chaque occasion et respectez ce budget. Cela vous aidera à prendre des décisions éclairées et à éviter les dépenses excessives.

2. Offrir des cadeaux faits maison : Les cadeaux faits maison ont

une valeur sentimentale et peuvent être très appréciés. Utilisez vos compétences et votre créativité pour créer des cadeaux uniques tels que des albums photo personnalisés, des biscuits faits maison, des objets d'artisanat ou des poèmes. Les cadeaux faits maison sont souvent moins chers que les cadeaux achetés en magasin, mais ils ont une valeur personnelle beaucoup plus grande.

3. Organiser des échanges de cadeaux : Au lieu d'acheter des cadeaux pour chaque personne lors des occasions spéciales en famille ou entre amis, organisez des échanges de cadeaux. Fixez un budget maximum pour les cadeaux et tirez au sort les noms des personnes à qui vous offrirez des cadeaux. Cela permet de réduire le nombre de cadeaux à acheter tout en préservant l'esprit de générosité et de célébration.

4. Faire des achats en avance : Anticipez les occasions spéciales et les anniversaires en faisant vos achats à l'avance. Lorsque vous tombez sur une bonne affaire ou un cadeau parfait pour quelqu'un, achetez-le et conservez-le pour l'occasion appropriée. Cela vous permettra d'économiser de l'argent et d'éviter de dépenser précipitamment à la dernière minute.

5. Utiliser des sites de bons plans et de codes promo : Consultez des sites web spécialisés dans les bons plans et les codes promo pour trouver des offres intéressantes sur les cadeaux et les articles de fête. De nombreux sites proposent des réductions exclusives, des codes promo ou des ventes flash qui vous permettent d'acheter des cadeaux à des prix réduits. Prenez le temps de rechercher et de comparer les prix avant de faire vos achats.

6. Offrir des expériences plutôt que des objets : Au lieu d'acheter des cadeaux matériels, envisagez d'offrir des expériences mémorables. Offrez des bons pour des activités telles qu'un dîner

au restaurant, une journée au spa, une sortie culturelle ou une escapade en week-end. Les expériences offrent des moments précieux et peuvent être moins coûteuses que l'achat de cadeaux physiques.

7. Réutiliser et recycler les emballages cadeaux : Ne gaspillez pas d'argent sur les emballages cadeaux coûteux et éphémères. Réutilisez les emballages cadeaux que vous avez déjà ou recyclez des matériaux tels que les journaux, les magazines ou les chutes de tissu pour créer vos propres emballages personnalisés et uniques.

8. Communiquer et partager vos intentions : Si vous souhaitez réduire les dépenses liées aux cadeaux et aux occasions spéciales, communiquez avec vos proches et partagez vos intentions. Expliquez que vous cherchez à économiser de l'argent et proposez des alternatives telles que des échanges de services, des moments de qualité passés ensemble ou des cadeaux symboliques. L'important est de célébrer les moments spéciaux et de montrer votre affection, peu importe le coût des cadeaux.

En mettant en pratique ces astuces, vous pouvez économiser sur les cadeaux et les occasions spéciales tout en préservant leur signification et leur importance. Établissez un budget, offrez des cadeaux faits maison, organisez des échanges de cadeaux et faites vos achats à l'avance. Utilisez des sites de bons plans, offrez des expériences, réutilisez les emballages cadeaux et communiquez avec vos proches. Rappelez-vous que l'intention et le geste sont plus importants que le coût d'un cadeau, et que les occasions spéciales peuvent être célébrées de manière significative et économique.

CHAPITRE 14 : ÉCONOMISER POUR L'AVENIR : CONSEILS EN MATIÈRE D'ÉPARGNE ET D'INVESTISSEMENT

L'épargne et l'investissement sont des éléments clés pour assurer votre sécurité financière à long terme. Dans ce chapitre, nous allons explorer différentes astuces et conseils pour vous aider à économiser pour l'avenir et à prendre des décisions éclairées en matière d'épargne et d'investissement.

1. Établir des objectifs financiers : Commencez par définir vos objectifs financiers à long terme. Que ce soit pour acheter une maison, constituer un fonds d'urgence ou préparer votre retraite, des objectifs clairs vous aideront à rester motivé et à orienter vos décisions financières.

2. Établir un budget : Un budget bien établi est la clé pour économiser de l'argent. Passez en revue vos revenus et vos

dépenses mensuelles, et identifiez les domaines où vous pouvez réduire vos dépenses. Fixez des limites pour vos dépenses discrétionnaires et allouez une partie de vos revenus à l'épargne et à l'investissement.

3. Créer un fonds d'urgence : Constituez un fonds d'urgence pour faire face aux imprévus tels que les frais médicaux, les réparations domiciliaires ou la perte d'emploi. Visez à économiser suffisamment pour couvrir au moins trois à six mois de dépenses courantes. Placez ce fonds dans un compte d'épargne liquide et facilement accessible.

4. Automatiser vos épargnes : Configurez des virements automatiques pour transférer une partie de vos revenus vers un compte d'épargne chaque mois. Cela vous aidera à épargner régulièrement sans effort supplémentaire. Traitez votre épargne comme une dépense incontournable et prioritaire.

5. Réduire les dettes : Éliminez les dettes à intérêt élevé le plus rapidement possible. Concentrez-vous sur le remboursement des cartes de crédit, des prêts personnels ou des prêts étudiants avec des taux d'intérêt élevés. Moins de dettes signifie moins d'intérêts à payer, ce qui vous permettra d'économiser davantage à long terme.

6. Diversifier vos investissements : Lorsque vous êtes prêt à investir, diversifiez votre portefeuille. Ne placez pas toutes vos économies dans un seul type d'investissement. Investissez dans différents secteurs, classes d'actifs et régions géographiques pour réduire les risques et maximiser les opportunités de rendement.

7. Explorer les options d'investissement : Renseignez-vous sur les différentes options d'investissement telles que les actions, les

obligations, les fonds communs de placement, les fonds indiciels, les ETF et l'immobilier. Consultez un conseiller financier ou faites vos propres recherches pour comprendre les avantages et les risques de chaque option et choisir celles qui correspondent à vos objectifs et à votre profil de risque.

8. Consulter un conseiller financier : Si vous avez besoin d'aide pour établir un plan financier solide, envisagez de consulter un conseiller financier qualifié. Un conseiller peut vous aider à définir vos objectifs, à élaborer une stratégie d'épargne et d'investissement, et à ajuster votre plan en fonction de votre situation personnelle.

9. Profiter des avantages fiscaux : Renseignez-vous sur les avantages fiscaux liés à l'épargne et à l'investissement, tels que les régimes de retraite individuels (REER) ou les comptes d'épargne libre d'impôt (CELI). Ces comptes offrent des avantages fiscaux qui peuvent vous aider à augmenter vos économies à long terme.

10. Faire un suivi régulier : Revoyez régulièrement vos progrès en matière d'épargne et d'investissement. Réévaluez vos objectifs, ajustez votre plan si nécessaire et assurez-vous que vos investissements sont en ligne avec vos objectifs et votre tolérance au risque.

En suivant ces conseils en matière d'épargne et d'investissement, vous pouvez mettre en place une stratégie financière solide pour l'avenir. Établissez des objectifs, créez un budget, constituez un fonds d'urgence et automatisez vos épargnes. Réduisez vos dettes, diversifiez vos investissements, explorez les options d'investissement et consultez un conseiller financier si nécessaire. Profitez des avantages fiscaux et suivez régulièrement vos progrès. Avec une approche réfléchie et proactive, vous pouvez prendre les bonnes décisions financières pour sécuriser votre avenir financier.

CHAPITRE 15 : CONCLUSION - ADOPTER UNE MENTALITÉ D'ÉCONOMIE AU QUOTIDIEN

Félicitations ! Vous avez parcouru ce livre qui regorge d'astuces et de conseils pour faire des économies au quotidien. Vous avez maintenant les connaissances nécessaires pour adopter une mentalité d'économie qui vous permettra de mieux gérer vos finances, de réaliser vos objectifs financiers et de vivre de manière plus consciente.

L'économie au quotidien ne signifie pas se priver de tout, mais plutôt prendre des décisions éclairées pour dépenser judicieusement son argent et maximiser ses ressources. Cela implique de repenser nos habitudes de consommation, de rechercher des alternatives économiques et de faire preuve de créativité pour économiser de l'argent sans pour autant sacrifier notre qualité de vie.

Au fil des chapitres, nous avons exploré différentes facettes de l'économie quotidienne, de la réduction des dépenses alimentaires à la gestion efficace du budget, en passant par les économies d'énergie, les achats en ligne, les dépenses liées au transport, les loisirs, les soins de beauté, les voyages, les vêtements, la santé, les cadeaux et les investissements. Vous avez appris à repérer les opportunités d'économies, à prendre des décisions réfléchies et à mettre en pratique des astuces simples pour économiser de l'argent dans tous les aspects de votre vie.

L'adoption d'une mentalité d'économie au quotidien vous permettra de réaliser de nombreux avantages. Tout d'abord, cela vous aidera à améliorer votre situation financière en réduisant vos dépenses et en épargnant davantage. Cela vous permettra également de vous libérer du stress financier, d'atteindre vos objectifs financiers à court et à long terme, et d'élaborer un plan solide pour votre avenir financier.

En adoptant une mentalité d'économie, vous développez également une conscience accrue de la valeur de l'argent et de la manière dont vous choisissez de le dépenser. Vous devenez plus conscient de vos habitudes de consommation, de vos besoins réels par rapport à vos désirs et de l'impact de vos choix financiers sur votre vie et sur l'environnement.

Cependant, il est important de noter que l'économie au quotidien ne doit pas devenir une obsession. Il est important de trouver un équilibre entre la gestion de vos finances et votre bien-être global. Il est tout à fait acceptable de vous accorder des plaisirs occasionnels et de profiter de la vie, tant que vous le faites de manière réfléchie et en tenant compte de votre situation financière.

Rappelez-vous également que l'économie au quotidien n'est pas une tâche isolée, mais plutôt un mode de vie. C'est un processus continu qui nécessite de la discipline, de la patience et de la persévérance. Continuez à vous informer, à chercher de nouvelles astuces d'économie et à adapter votre approche en fonction de votre évolution personnelle et de vos objectifs.

En conclusion, adopter une mentalité d'économie au quotidien est un choix puissant qui peut avoir un impact significatif sur votre vie financière et sur votre bien-être général. En mettant en pratique les conseils de ce livre,

vous êtes en bonne voie pour vivre de manière plus consciente, économique et épanouissante. Alors, n'attendez plus, prenez les rênes de vos finances et construisez un avenir financièrement sécurisé et équilibré. Bonne route vers une vie d'économie au quotidien !

www.ingramcontent.com/pod-product-compliance
Lightning Source LLC
Chambersburg PA
CBHW070858220526
45466CB00005B/2038

Quick Guide To
Brain Meditation

Anura Gurugé

Edition One
December 2016

WOWNH LLC
New Hampshire
USA
www.wownh.com

First published by WOWNH LLC in November 2016.

ISBN-10: 1540551296
ISBN-13: 978-1540551290

Printed in the United States of America

This book is printed on acid-free paper.

PHOTOGRAPHIC CREDITS: All of the images used in this book, including that on the cover, are public domain material (from the likes of Wikipedia) or photographs taken by the author (an avid photographer).

To

You and Your Amazing Brain

You Are What Transpires
In **Your** Brain,

What Transpires
In **Your** Brain Is **You**.

Furthering & Fostering
This Wonderful
Oneness.

Brain Meditation

Meditation Through Contemplation

Brain Meditation.

Think, meditation.

Think Meditation.

Befriending Your Brain	Brain Meditation

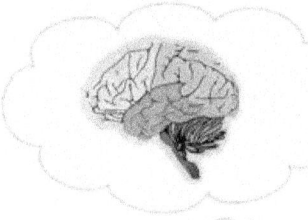

Two Processes, One Goal:
Melding YOU With Your Brain

GENUINE

< Productivity >   < Contentment >   < Serenity >

At A Minimum

Please refer to the summaries & keywords/phrases
at the end of each chapter to gain an initial high-level
perspective into this self-help program --
in addition to looking at chapters 1 & 2.

The Primary Techniques Of
This Self-Help Program

Befriending Your Brain	Brain Meditation

❖ Morning ritual

❖ Frequent *'how are things'* pings

❖ Maintaining awareness of brain

❖ Night ritual

❖ *'Virtualization'*
(a.k.a. 'visualization')

❖ Mindful thinking
 ✓ Thinking for pleasure
 ✓ Thinking for relaxation

Smile,
often & with feeling

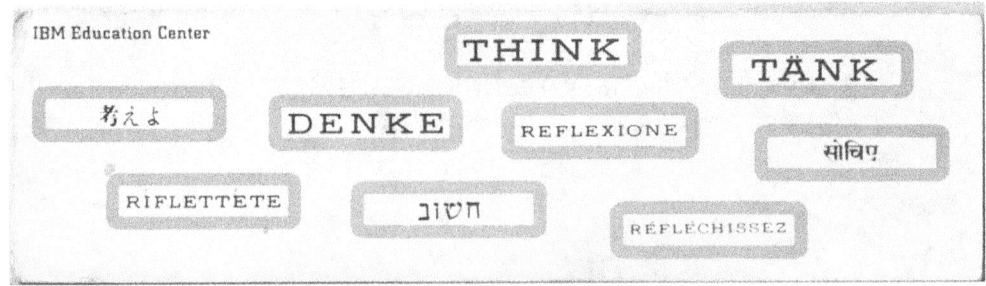

The paper **'Think'** sign I received upon joining IBM (the then tech titan) in August 1974.

Four decades later it is still on my desk, under my main PC monitor.

It is a constant inspiration.

Thinking is the way we interact with our brain. As such thinking plays a major role when it comes to 'Brain Meditation'.
'Brain Meditation' is realized via various 'forms' of thinking.
That, if you think about it, makes sense.
Anything to do with the brain involves 'thinking'.
All forms of meditation, in one way or another',
call for 'focus'.
Again, if you think about it, you will appreciate that
'focus' is but another word for 'thinking'!

THINK.

It can, and it will, change your life
-- for the better.

This book, as a '*Quick Guide*',
is an adjunct to the author's
much more detailed and lengthy
'Brain Meditation --
For True Productivity & Serenity'.

This book, nonetheless, is a complete,
self-contained, stand-alone text.
You can learn and master
"Brain Meditation"
with just this book.
You **do not** need the bigger book.

However, if you seek more detail,
further explanations, background,
rationales, or context, you should
consider reading the other book
which is available both in
printed and eBook versions
(from Amazon for a start).

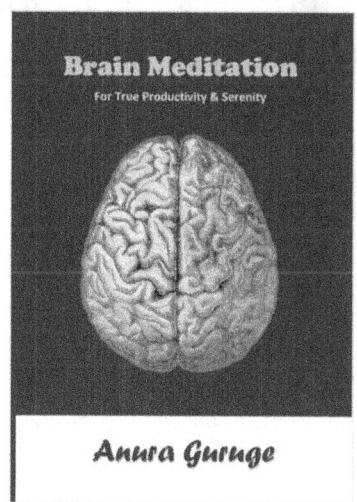

Meditation is all in the mind.

Hence, your brain is central
to any form of meditation.

'Brain meditation'
cuts to the chase; goes to the source.

Just you & your brain
-- in oneness.

Focused, concerted meditation,
on-the-go, in background-mode,
with the focus very much
on '**you**', '**you**' alone,
and '**your**' future.

CONTENTS

Preface xvii

The Five Precepts Of 'Brain Meditation' xx

The Seven Daily Disciplines Of 'Brain Meditation' xxi

1. High-Level Overview 1

2. Introduction 3
   Summary: The Introduction 11
   Keywords & Phrases From 'The Introduction' 13

3. Befriending Your Brain 14
   Summary: Befriending Your Brain 21
   Keywords & Phrases From 'Befriending Your Brain' 23

4. Brain Meditation 24
   Summary: Brain Meditation 34
   Keywords & Phrases From 'Brain Meditation' 36

5. Various Forms Of Thinking 37
   Summary: Various Forms Of Thinking 45
   Keywords & Phrases From 'Various Forms Of Thinking' 47

6. Power Thinking 48
   Summary: Power Thinking 54
   Keywords & Phrases From 'Power Thinking' 56

7. Process, Schedule & Expectations 57
   Keywords & Phrases From 'Process, Schedule & Expectations' .. 59

8. Results, Rewards & Risks 60
   Keywords & Phrases From 'Results, Rewards & Risks' 66

9. The Thinking You 67
   Keywords & Phrases From 'The Thinking You' 71

Partial Index 73

Note the '**Summary**' and '**Keywords & Phrases**' at chapter end.

PREFACE

"The purpose of meditation is personal transformation."

-- Henepola Gunaratana
(Sri Lankan Buddhist monk)

This is a self-help book – in *'quick guide'* form. It deals with a new, very modern and atypical form of meditation -- *meditation that can be done in background mode.* It, as such, does not require any dedicated time. It is, therefore, ideally suited for the time constraints of today's 'mobile age'. This meditation is called 'brain meditation' -- because it is so centered on the brain. It is all achieved through 'thinking'. Thinking which is done while doing routine, mundane tasks such as: brushing your teeth, getting a cup of coffee or doing some exercise. [*There is a pictorial diagram in chapter 2.*] Hence, it is easy to practice. Furthermore, it is easy to learn and master.

'Brain meditation', as spelled out in this quick guide, will help you attain oneness with your brain. There are manifold tangible benefits to this 'oneness'; a prevailing sense of inner serenity being one. Chapters 8 & 9 talk about the rewards (and the marginal potential risks) of this program. You can, by all means, *skip ahead* and have a look. Actually, you can go ahead and riffle through this book -- *at will.* I wrote it such that you can skim through it, initially, without having to read it, sequentially, page-by-page. The chapter titles should assist you with the navigation. The *'Summary'* and *'Keywords & Phrases'* pages found at the conclusion of the chapters will, in addition, provide you with a good 'first-cut' overview of what this program is all about.

I tried to make this book as pithy as possible. I made a point of using a lot of bullet points, short paragraphs and summary pages. My hope is that this will help you grasp what 'brain meditation' is all about -- without having to read too many words.

Yes, I have previously published a longer, more detailed and possibly a tad verbose book on this subject (in September 2016). It is titled *"Brain Meditation – For True Productivity & Serenity"*, and is available in both printed and eBook form. Those of you who want a deeper understanding of this subject, particularly in terms of the rationale, background and merits, should consult that book. I realized the need for a shorter and more bullet point-oriented *'quick guide'* as I was nearing the end of that larger work. This is that *'quick guide'*.

You can learn and master 'brain meditation' using just this book – and nothing else.

'Brain meditation' is surprisingly non-onerous. It is so non-onerous that you may, at first, be skeptical. You may find it hard to believe that you can indeed meditate, without having to sit cross-legged, in a darkened room sans distraction. But, the truth is that meditation is between you and your brain. (Some prefer to think of it in terms of you and your mind – and this is addressed in chapter 2.) This book is all about how you can very effectively meditate, in background mode, via mindful thinking – i.e., by engaging your brain in thought. Hence, *'brain meditation'* as opposed to *'meditation for the brain'*.

The focus of this book is your brain, and your relationship with your brain. This book urges you to pay attention to your brain and maintain an awareness of your brain. The two words you will come across most often within this book are: **'Think'** and **'Smile'**. Neither of which is a bad for you. {*SMILE*} In fact, there is nothing in this book that will do you any harm: mentally, physically, emotionally or financially. 'Brain meditation' has no religious connotations or basis, whatsoever. It is totally independent of religion, belief systems and cultures. It is extremely inclusive, with nary an exclusion. It is open to all, and all can benefit, equally.

This is my 26th published book as a sole author. I have long given up on writing in the hope of fame or fortune. I wrote this book to _help you_. I have been successfully practicing 'brain meditation' for over 40-years. It has served me well. I, as such, want to share it with you – mainly because it can be so effective, despite being disarmingly simple and easy.

I am not a doctor, a psychologist or a therapist. By training I am a computer scientist with a Master's in that discipline. But, in the end, I consider myself a writer and hence why I wrote this book. That, in my opinion, is what writers are supposed to do. {*SMILE*} And to be fair, there is also the matter of my name. My surname is *'Guruge'*. You can see that the first part is *'guru'*, i.e., the Asian term for a teacher or guide. The latter part, the *'ge'*, pronounced *'ghay'*, means 'house'. So, my last name denotes that I am *'from the house of the teacher'*. Well, as you know, meditation is often associated with *'Gurus'*. Hence, who better to write an introductory book on a new form of meditation?

'Typo' is my middle name and as such *you should* feel cheated if this book was, miraculously, devoid of any typos – despite many efforts to catch as many as we can. {*SMILE*} If the typos bother you please return the book and ask for your money back, in full. Ideally, do so after you have finished reading it in its entirety – or have read enough to help you embark on 'brain meditation'.

I am extremely confident that this book will _help you_ – as it is meant to do. I would not have written it otherwise. So, I now wish you _bon chance_ and _happy thinking._ May your brain be with you hereinafter. _Pax._

Anura Gurugé
Lakes Region, New Hampshire,
November 2016

"Your brain is yours and yours alone.

No one but no one can take it away from you

(ill-health an exception, but that is still you).

Even in the darkest of times,

you will always have your brain.

You can always find solace

in your brain."

THE FIVE PRECEPTS OF 'BRAIN MEDITATION'

1. 'Brain meditation' is all *about you*, your brain, and your future.

2. 'Brain meditation' only involves *mindful thinking* and lots of smiling.

3. 'Brain meditation' only requires you to *commune* regularly with your brain.

4. 'Brain meditation' is meant to be done in *background mode*.

5. 'Brain meditation' is as *inclusive* as possible.

THE SEVEN DAILY DISCIPLINES OF 'BRAIN MEDITATION'

'Befriending the brain'/maintaining friendship

1. *Good morning* ritual.

2. 'Touching base' with your brain (i.e., *pinging* brain) at least 10 times a day, ideally more.

3. Maintaining constant *awareness* of your brain.

4. *Good night* ritual.

'Brain meditation' component

5. Regular *virtualization* throughout the day.

6. Mindful thinking, in the form of *personal thinking*, whenever.

Feel good aspect

7. *Smiling*, as much as you can.

1.
HIGH-LEVEL OVERVIEW

✿ 'Brain meditation' is a modern, *background mode*, do it *on-the-fly* (e.g., while brushing your teeth) meditation technique, for today's *mobile age* -- that does not require any dedicated time, nor the need to sit cross-legged.

✿ 'Brain meditation' relies, entirely, on various forms of mindful thinking, on a regular basis, to focus, center and calm your brain – and as such, also you.

✿ Routinely focusing, centering and calming your brain will help you to relieve stress, 'remotivate' your inner self, stay on an even keel, sharpen your thinking, and smile more often.

✿ Brain meditation' is extremely *you-centric*, with much of the mindful thinking you are urged to do (known as virtualization) involving just you, your life and your future.

✿ As with exercise and some other forms of meditation, the mindful thinking activities of 'brain meditation' stimulate the brain to produce more of the body's naturally occurring 'feel good' chemicals, e.g., dopamine.

✿ 'Brain meditation' will strengthen, finesse, deepen and make more intimate your relationship with your brain.

✿ There are two (2) aspects to 'brain meditation': 'befriending your brain' which fosters oneness with the brain, and mindful thinking (which, in the main, is the meditating part).

- ⚙ Your befriended brain will be your best, most loyal, reliable and trusted friend for life; always there for you, eager to support you in all your endeavors, and capable of bailing you out 'in a jam'.

- ⚙ 'Brain meditation' is not onerous in that it is all done in your mind while you get on with your normal life – and it makes no demands at all on your body, your wallet, your wardrobe, your beliefs, nor your mental wellbeing.

- ⚙ Much of the meditation *per se* is realized via (so called) *virtualizations* – which focus and relax your brain, many times a day, through a process of taking fleeting mental breaks to quickly look ahead *'to the next couple of hours'*.

- ⚙ 'Brain meditation', which only involves **thinking** & **smiling** is very much a win-win proposition with negligible risks.

- ⚙ 'Brain meditation', in time, will make you into a **THINKING YOU**, more: thoughtful, mindful, considerate, perspicacious, empowered and serene.

THINK

SMILE

2.
INTRODUCTION

'Brain meditation' is a very pure and concentrated form of meditation. As such it is extremely effective. It does away with anything and everything superfluous and intervening. It is devoid of 'frills' or affectations.

'Brain meditation' is a technique that is focused, 100% of the time, laser-sharp, on the core of every form of meditation – i.e., *your brain*. Hence the name, *brain meditation*. Much of what constitutes 'brain meditation' is done via *mindful thinking*. Thinking being our best (if not only) way of engaging with our brain.

> ➤ 'Brian meditation' is meditation through contemplation. ◄

It is meditation based upon thinking. Think, meditation → THINK meditation.

Many of the activities involved in 'brain meditation' can be shown to be effective triggers that stimulate the brain to produce *'happy chemicals'*; *dopamine*, the body's 'feel good' chemical, being one. *[See figure below.]*

Meditation is all in the mind. Every form of meditation, in the end, in one way or another, involves the mind. Wikipedia's entry for meditation, citing a 2008 scientific paper, starts off with: '*Meditation is a practice where an individual trains the mind …*'. Meditation is about getting your mind to focus, pushing aside distractions and concentrating on a specific goal.

The true essence of any sort of meditation is that of you *communing* with your mind. In other words, you having an intimate and 'deep' conversation with your mind. This communing, between you and your mind, is what meditating is all about. Period. So, meditating, cut to the chase, is about having *meaningful, private moments with you mind*. That is it. Nothing more, nothing less. And 'brain meditation' capitalizes on that.

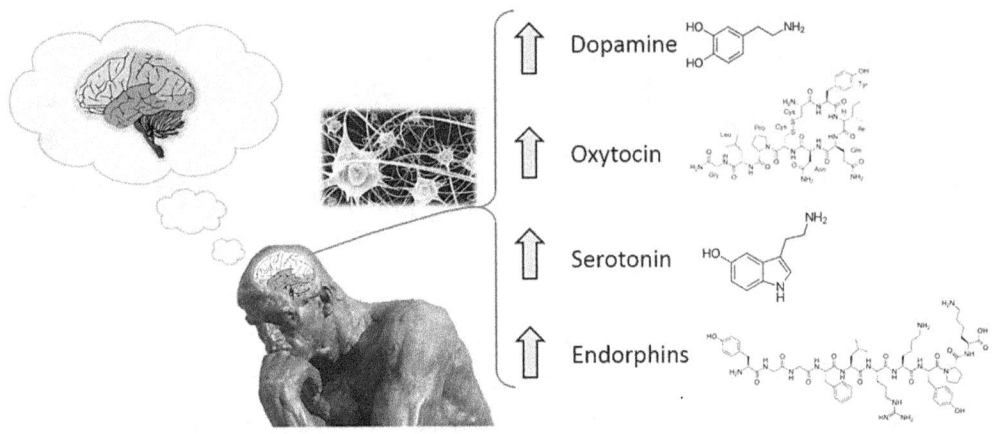

Brain's chief *'feel good'* chemicals

Some of the chemistry behind 'brain meditation'.

The 'Mind' vs. 'Brain' Conundrum

What we perceive as our 'mind', in the end, is in some way centered (if not totally contained) within our brain. Our nervous system, essentially a very sophisticated wiring harness, is an extension of the brain; the tentacles of the brain reaching out into the body's extremities. Without a brain to interpret, monitor and control it, the nervous system cannot do much.

Whether you like it or not, your brain is the only organ in your body that has the capability and capacity to do any 'information (or signal) processing'. It is, to the extent of our current scientific understanding, the only organ that possesses **'thinking'** (i.e., cognitive) powers. In other words, as far as we can tell, our brain is the only known 'computer' we have inside our body.

Maybe, you don't want to fully accept that our 'mind' has to be contained within our brain. Nonetheless, in the end, you still will have to concede that much of the so called mental faculties of the mind have to be handled by the brain. Let's just agree, so that it does not become a sticking point, that at least *70%* of 'the mind' must in some way be related to the brain. And that is good enough.

We can now proceed on the understanding that there is a definite overlap, of at least 70%, between our mind and our brain. So, feel free to substitute *mind* in place of *brain*, when we are talking about 'brain meditation'-- if that will help you relate better.

In the remainder of this book, please note, that when I talk about *'the brain'* I am also referring to *'the mind'*.

The Brain < = > The Mind

Types Of Meditation & Religious Connotations

There are many different types of meditation; 23 such types per Google.

A key differentiator between these various types has to do with 'focus' – i.e., how and what you concentrate on. There are two distinct categories: *'focused attention meditation'* and *'open monitoring meditation'*. With *'focused attention'*, per the name, you are expected to focus on one specific entity. It could be your breathing, something you chant, a soothing mental image, or a physical object (e.g., a flower).

'Open monitoring', on the other hand, permits you to keep an open mind to experience other 'things' around you as you meditate.

There is also *'walking meditation'*. The act of walking providing the focus, i.e., the 'grounding', for meditation.

The takeaway here is that there is no one specific means, methodology or technique when it comes to meditation.

There is, furthermore, nothing, whatsoever, that dictates that you have to: adopt a certain pose, sit in a quietened room, wear designer yoga pants, focus on your breathing, visualize a calming scene, chant *'OM'* repetitively, or use finger cymbals.

In reality you can very effectively meditate anytime, anywhere, as long as you are able to establish and maintain a strong, focused bond with your brain.

Period.

The ability to meditate on the fly, by forming a strong bond with your brain, is the basis of 'brain meditation'.

Meditation transcends religion.

Meditation is not specific to Eastern religions, e.g., Buddhism or Hinduism. Meditation predates even these ancient religions. It was practiced in the west in antiquity, in particular by the Greeks, totally divorced of any eastern influences.

'Brain meditation' *is totally independent of any religion, belief system or appreciation of spirituality.* 'Brain meditation' is more like an exercise regimen – a daily, *gentle*, non-stressful exercise regimen for the brain.

The Basics Of 'Brain Meditation'

o 'Brain meditation' relies on focusing, centering (i.e., 'grounding') and calming your brain, for very short bursts of time, on a regular basis – throughout the day.

o This process of focusing, centering and calming your brain is done through *mindful* (or *conscious*) **thinking**.

o A key form of mindful thinking involved is referred to as *virtualization* – though you can also think of it as *visualization*.

The two words *virtualization* and *visualization* are interchangeable, and you can, in your mind, chose whichever that works the best for you.

o Virtualization requires you to spend **a few seconds at a time**, through the course of the day, whenever and wherever you can, thinking of *yourself in the future*.

Virtualization is all about YOU and your future.

So, a large part of 'brain meditation' consists of you proactively thinking about your future. It is a way of projecting yourself into the future, within your mind.

o Virtualization is meant to be done in *timeshare mode*, i.e., while you are physically engaged doing something else.

It can thus be done, very effectively, while you are: brushing your teeth, waiting in line to get a coffee, taking a shower (or bath), sitting in a waiting room, visting the bathroom, shaving (your legs, face or both), sitting at traffic lights … *[See figure below.]*

o Virtualization serves two purposes.

1. Doing a virtualization, even though it is but for a few seconds, focuses, grounds and calms your brain/mind. That is key. Doing this at least 10 times a day starts to add up. It is cumulative.

2. Virtualization helps you to better deal with your future. With virtualization you have already looked ahead. You have established some expectations. You now face the future with more confidence and less anxiety. This is one of the ways that 'brain meditation', in time, brings calmness and serenity into your life.

o 'Brain meditation', unlike most other forms of meditation, does not require any dedicated, meditation-only time.

It, with virtualization at its core, can and should be done in background, multitasking mode. This is the beauty of 'brain meditation'. It can be done, very successfully, in a non-intrusive, seamless manner, as a part of your everyday life. You do not have to allocate any time or place to do it. It can be done on the fly as you get on with your life.

o Other forms of mindful, *purposeful thinking*, if you have the time, can augment virtualization and further strengthen your 'brain meditation' regimen and experience.

While it is important to give your brain some 'comfort breaks' it is best to <u>minimize</u> downtime/idle time (during waking hours). Try to always indulge in some form of mindful thinking that focuses and centers your brain. That is an aspect of 'brain meditation'. *Mindful thinking will always be calming.*

o Before you can embark on 'brain meditation' you have to **befriend your brain.**

Befriending your brain means that you (while awake) establish and maintain a constant awareness of your brain.

It means that you start thinking of, and dealing with, your brain as if it was your best friend.

The *befriending* aspect is based on regular, very short duration, *pings* with your brain – i.e., *'hi, how are you'* interactions that should take less than two seconds to complete.

o This program urges you to **SMILE**, and to smile often, and do so with feeling. That alone will make you feel good, and, furthermore, make those that see you feel good too!

Just some of the times/places you can
virtualize or indulge in some mindful thinking.

<u>*Main Characteristics Of* 'Brain Meditation'</u>

o 'Brain meditation', per its name, is all about very specific, direct interactions
   with your brain on a regular, routine basis.

o 'Brain meditation' does not require any dedicated time.

o 'Brain meditation' can be done on the fly, in timeshare mode as you go
   about your life.

o 'Brain meditation' is very much about you, you alone, and your future. Its
   focus is <u>you</u>. You meditate by thinking about yourself and your anticipated
   future.

o 'Brain meditation' does not require you to sit or stand in any particular way,
   chant anything, breathe in a regulated manner, close your eyes, light any
   candles, burn any incense, listen to any music, or wear any special clothing.

o 'Brain meditation' *requires that you are ever aware that you have a brain!*

o   'Brain meditation' is based on the notion of *oneness with one's brain.*

o   'Brain meditation' is easy to learn, practice and master – though it will take some time before <u>you realize</u> that it is indeed working, and that it is slowly transforming you into a calmer, less anxious, self-assured YOU.

o   'Brain meditation' relies on you spending as much time as you can (while awake) engaged in mindful and purposeful thinking -- virtualization being just one aspect. Mindful thinking of any form, whether it is for problem solving, business needs or for pleasure can focus and center your brain – thus serving as meditation time.

o   'Brain meditation', like some other forms of meditation, involves many activities that (just like exercise and yoga) are known to encourage the brain to produce more **'feel good' chemicals/hormones.** *Dopamine*, the chemical that controls the brain's *reward mechanism*, is key among these. But, as with some other forms of meditation, it is believed that 'brain meditation' stimulates the production of **serotonin, oxytocin** and **endorphins**, all which are known to make you feel good and content.

o   'Brain meditation' does not claim to increase your **inborn IQ** – i.e., the intelligence profile and limits you were born with. It will, however, definitely help you better utilize the IQ you *already possess* but are not using to its full capacity. In other words, it will *fine-tune* the IQ you currently have so as to make it sharper and more acute. If you think of your brain as an engine, 'brain meditation' will ensure that it works as efficiently as possible, thus delivering close to its max output. But, you are still working with the engine you already possessed. 'Brain meditation' will NOT replace that existing engine with a bigger, more powerful engine.

Refer to the *'Results, Rewards & Risks'* chapter, i.e., chapter 8, to learn what you should gain from this self-help program. You will also get assurance that there are no major risks or downsides involved.

A Few Points To Keep In Mind

Just because it does not ask for you to devote any specific time for meditation, sit crossed legged, close your eyes, or chant obscure Sanskrit words, does not mean that 'Brain meditation' is not *bona fide* meditation. If anything, it is a more concerted and concentrated form of meditation than most other forms.

It is one of the purest forms of meditation – direct, intense interaction between you and your brain/mind.

'Brain meditation' via *virtualization* will become your preferred (and treasured) go-to security blanket!

One of the ultimate goals of 'brain meditation' is to imbue you with a deep-seated sense of **serenity**.

SMILE. *Smile often*. Smiling is good for you. This program advocates exuberant smiling.

Summary: The Introduction

ೞ 'Brain meditation' is a very pure, concentrated and *effective* form of meditation that sets out to create *"oneness with one's brain"*.

ೞ 'Brain meditation', via *mindful thinking*, relies on focusing your brain – via regular, direct and very specific interactions with your brain.

ೞ Any and all forms of meditation involve the mind – and there is an undeniable connection between your brain and your mind. *The Brain < => The Mind.*

ೞ The brain is the only organ in the body capable of processing information, emotions & feelings.

ೞ Meditation transcends religion and there are many, many different forms of meditation.

ೞ 'Brain meditation' focuses, centers and calms your brain, in regular short bursts, throughout the day.

ೞ *Virtualization/visualization*, the bedrock of 'brain meditation', is based on you thinking of *yourself in the future*, multiple times a day, whenever you can.

ೞ Virtualization, and as such 'brain meditation', is meant to be done in *timeshare mode.*

ೞ Virtualization serves two purposes: 1/ focuses, grounds and calms the brain & 2/ helps you better *cope with future events.*

ೞ *Befriending your brain* is a prerequisite to 'brain meditation' because you need to be always aware that you have a brain.

ೞ 'Brain meditation' helps you better utilize your *inborn IQ* by *fine-tuning* your brain. It does not make any claims to being able to increase the IQ profile/limits you were born with.

ೞ Many of the benefits experienced with 'brain meditation' can be directly attributed to the fact that 'brain meditation', just like exercise, yoga and some other forms of meditation, stimulates the brain to produce more

dopamine, etc. – the brain chemicals associated with all aspects of bodily *well-being*.

ɕ₃ 'Brain meditation' expects you to spend as much time as you can on *mindful/purposeful thinking*.

ɕ₃ 'Brain meditation' urges you to **SMILE** and to smile with feeling as much as you can.

"You can very effectively meditate anytime, anywhere as long as you are able to establish and maintain a strong, focused bond with your brain."

"Meditation is a practice where an individual trains the mind …" – Wikipedia

Benjamin Franklin, Philadelphia

Keywords & Phrases From 'The Introduction'

- ✓ Oneness with one's brain.

- ✓ Virtualization – Visualization.

- ✓ Mindful thinking.

- ✓ Communing.

- ✓ Contemplation.

- ✓ Befriending the brain.

- ✓ Aware of your brain.

- ✓ Only organ that can think.

- ✓ Transcends religion.

- ✓ Not trying to increase inborn IQ.

- ✓ Fine-tuning brain.

- ✓ Increase efficiency of the existing 'engine'.

- ✓ Meditation in timeshare mode.

- ✓ Own personal security blanket.

- ✓ Focus, centered and ground.

- ✓ **Dopamine.**

- ✓ Serenity.

- ✓ YOU.

- ✓ Your future.

- ✓ **SMILE.**

3.
BEFRIENDING
YOUR BRAIN

Did you start *today*, first thing in the morning, by bidding a cheery *'Good Morning'* to your brain? If not, why not? Have you had a falling out with your brain? Given all that it does for you, with very little thanks from you, shouldn't you at least wish it *good morning*? It is actually very easy to do, and you can do it without moving your lips.

If you work shifts or are a night-owl, you can flip *good morning* to *good evening* or *good night* for the duration of this book. Just use what is right for you. I use *good morning* per the 'majority rules' basis.

If you have not as yet greeted your brain today, please say a *good morning, good afternoon, good evening,* or *good day* to your brain right now. Don't be shy. Nobody can see or hear you. You are talking to your brain. You never have to say anything out aloud.

Your brain knows you. You are not strangers. Far from it. Your brain knows and understands *you* better than anybody else! We are trying to complete the other leg of this relationship. Get *you* to know your brain, very well, and to be aware of it at all times.

Some of you may find it helpful, when dealing with *you* and *your brain* to think of the *you* entity as either **your consciousness** or your tangible (*corporeal*) '*body*' . *Refer to the 'duality' section later in this chapter.* So, if it helps:

'you' and 'your brain' ⬄
'you' and 'your *consciousness*' / 'your *corporeal body*'

The *good morning* with your brain is pretty important when it comes to *befriending your brain*. Befriending is a two-way relationship; a friendship that has to be cultivated and nurtured.

Without *befriending* you and your brain are not truly connected, or in-synch. Befriending will give you the oneness with you brain that we seek. This oneness is key to everything we are trying to achieve – serenity the ultimate goal.

Starting now your brain is going to become your best friend – your best friend for life.

Your brain shares your body, your brain shares your life. Your brain is pretty important to your life; it dictates the quality of your life. Hence, the need to *befriend*.

That is why you need to *befriend your brain*.

> ➢ **Befriending your brain *will forever change your life.*** ◄

The Befriending & Nurturing Process

The process for befriending your brain, and then maintaining that close friendship, for life, involves **four (4)** *daily activities* that have to be performed (every day) *without fail*.

1. **'Good morning' ritual:** Start each day, first thing, as you are opening your eyes, by saying *'good morning'* to your brain. It does not have to be said out loud. You say it in your mind. This *'good morning'* serves as your way of checking-in with your brain. Telling your brain that you are ready, *with its help and support*, to start and confront the day.

2. **'Good night' ritual:** You end each day, as you are trying to get to sleep, eyes closed, by wishing your brain a very *'good night'*. You also thank it for all its invaluable help and support during the day. Savor and linger over this. Feel close to your brain. Seek oneness with your brain.

   The Day's Highlights: After saying the good night, eyes now closed, trying to fall asleep, start thinking, as mellow as you can, about all the *good things* that happened to you during the day. Even if you had a really bad day, there always has to be some good bits in each and every day. If nothing else, that you are going to sleep, at the end of a day, is a good thing in its own right. But, you will be able to find others. Stay mellow. I call this the compiling the *day's highlights reel*. Just keep on trying to think of all the good things in your life and what makes you content and happy. Do this: eyes closed, trying to fall asleep. In time, with daily practice, you will discover that this should help you find sleep.

Sweet Dreams: Doing the 'highlights' routine is not mandatory. You can still befriend your brain and do 'brain meditation' without the nightly highlights. The highlights routine, however, can be very soothing, helping you fall asleep easier, and influencing the content and tone of your dreams. You must know that all your dreams are created and directed by your brain. Your brain is trying to communicate with you, while you sleep, via your dreams.

Once you have befriended your brain you will, in time, start to notice that the nature and tenor of your dreams have changed – for the better. Your dreams will become mellower, more narrative, and closer to your real, day-to-day life. Following the befriending the relationship between you and your brain changes – positively. Your brain rather than wanting to shock you with bad dreams will, instead, try to be *'friendly & nice'* by sharing pleasant, story-like dreams with you.

Befriend your brain, do 'brain meditation' daily, and within six months to a year you will start noticing that your dreams have changed. Doing the *highlights reel* will help and expedite this change.

3. ***Ping* your brain at least 10 times a day:** You need to *touch base* with your brain, for no more than *two seconds* at a time, at least ten times a day – ideally much more; maybe twice an hour while awake. [You do not need to touch base with your brain while asleep. The brain will take care of maintaining your relationship while you sleep – your dreams playing an important role in this.]

These regular, routine *pings* (as I call them) does not have to be elaborate or verbose. Just a very quick: *"hi, how is it going?"*, *"how am **I** doing?"*, *"what's cooking?"*, *"I have not forgotten about you"*, *"so far so good … right?"* or *"thanks for everything"*. The words and sentiments are for <u>you</u> to choose. Do what you would with a friend. Think of it as texting your brain.

Two seconds is often marked out as: *Mississippi one, Mississippi two*. You can find, irrespective of how crazy busy your daily schedule might be, two seconds each hour. (Ideally you find four seconds per hour.) You can do the brain *pings* while you walk, go to the bathroom, reach out for a drink, scratch your head …

You just have to 'touch base' with your brain at least once each hour. Ideally more. But, once an hour is a great start.

In time you will come to look forward to these hourly *pings*! They can be very soothing. Why? Because these *pings* will trigger your brain into releasing *'good' chemicals* into your blood stream -- **dopamine**, the 'feel good' neurotransmitter, chief among them. But, it is believed that 'brain meditation' stimulates your brain into producing more **serotonin**, **oxytocin** and **endorphins** as well. It is these chemicals that make you *feel good*, *content*, *rewarded* and motivate you to **come back for more**. With our befriended brain, these regular *pings* will also make you feel content and centered. It all makes sense if you think about it. **You are activating 'happy chemicals' in your brain.**

4. **Never lose awareness of your (amazing) brain:** It should be like the relationship that mothers have with their children. You should never lose *sight* of your brain. In addition to the (mandatory) *pings*, whenever you get a brief mental respite during the day, think of your brain – with appreciation and gratitude. Just form a quick mental picture of you and your brain. Very quick. Under two seconds. *Mississippi one, Mississippi two.*

Come up with a mental image, a metaphor, an icon or even a 'feeling' by which you can relate to your brain. Totally up to you. Your own personal way of thinking about your brain. Use that *imagery* when you think about your brain. Yes, it is 'ok' to have multiple images and to use different ones at different times.

You can do this anywhere, anytime (and nobody will know you are doing it). You can do it while you take a shower. You can do it while brushing your teeth or combing your hair. You can do it while waiting for an elevator. You can do it while waiting for a cup of coffee, or waiting for the lights to change. *Just spare a fleeting/flashing thought for your brain.* That is it. That is all.

Thus, the **must do** four (4) daily activities are:

1. Good morning ritual.

2. Regular, routine *pings*.

3. Maintaining awareness of your brain, *at all times*.

4. Good night ritual.

<u>*Saying 'No' To Willpower*</u>

With the befriended brain we do away, altogether, with any notions of an imbalance in power or any inequality of 'wills'. Going forward there is only, ever, total harmony between you and your brain. Never a struggle. Never! It is always you and your brain working together in concert. 'Willpower' is a bad (banned) word you will never use again. Substitute *willingness* for 'willpower'.

As of now, everything to do with your brain is about *cooperation, collaboration* and *camaraderie*. These are the three *Cs* that characterize the relationship you will cultivate with your brain.

So, if there are lifestyle changes you want to make, e.g., dieting, regular exercise, giving up smoking, etc., you talk to your brain about what you want to achieve. You ask your brain for help. You ask your brain for active cooperation. And you don't do this just once. You have an ongoing dialog, multiple times a day. You solicit support from your brain. It becomes a part of your daily, routine interactions with your brain. OK?

<u>*The You And Your Brain 'Duality'*</u>

At one level you know and appreciate that you and your brain are indivisible. A viable, meaningful life is only possible together. That is a given.

However, as you have already seen, the befriending aspect of 'brain meditation' relies on you thinking of yourself and your brain as **two separate entities**. This is, however, but a mental artifact – one meant to help us establish a better 'oneness' between our **consciousness** (or at another level, our **corporeal body**) and our brain. Basically, we are making a distinction between the *'talking-walking-feeling-eating'* bodily us and our *'thinking-controlling-subconscious'* brain. I am very sure you understand what I am getting at – and the distinction.

When it comes to 'brain meditation' and 'befriending the brain' we need to be able to think and visualize our brain as a separate (*able to talk to*) entity. We do not have to make a big deal about this. Just deal with it as a 'device' we use to help us better commune with our brain. OK?

Christianity has the *Trinity*. We, when it comes to 'brain meditation', have a *duality*.

The notion of a *shoulder angel* may also help in coming to terms with this duality. The 'shoulder angel' is the goody two-shoes, saintly angel, always dressed in white, that sits on one's right shoulder. It is the 'angel' that does its utmost to dissuade us from succumbing to the evil temptations being suggested by the evil 'devil', dressed in red, perched on our left shoulder. That should serve as a good visual. 'You' on one side and 'your brain' on the other. Though in our case, there is definitely no 'bad' involved. Both sides, i.e., 'you' and 'your brain', are both good. Angelic, if you prefer. OK?

Creating this duality will do you no harm. It will certainly *NOT* make you schizophrenic! Because here is the ultimate irony. Though you are utilizing a duality to help you achieve it, what you are doing is *strengthening the ONENESS between you and your brain.* You are not trying to cleave the two apart. You are always trying to *bring them closer together – in* **constant communion**.

And this communing between you and your brain is always done internally, within yourself, with no mumbling or anything said out aloud. It is always private and personal. Just you and your brain. Nobody else needs to know. Nobody else will know – unless you decide to tell them.

A Few Additional Thoughts

We, in general, do not spend enough time thinking about our brain. We tend to ignore and take our brain for granted. That is a huge mistake. By befriending our brain we are going to rectify that.

We also, if *you think about it*, don't pay enough attention to our thinking! In other words, we don't make enough of an effort to think about what we are thinking. We need to rectify that. *We are, henceforth, going to think about thinking!* We are going to practice *mindful thinking* – or *conscious thinking.*

The primary theme of 'brain meditation' boils down to:
THINK. THINK. THINK.

Thinking is how we connect and interact with our brain.

Talking to your brain, with or without moving your lips, is also a form of thinking.

In this the *befriending* chapter, the emphasis is on thinking about <u>*your*</u> brain.

'Brain meditation' revolves around you, <u>daily</u>, multiple times a day, thinking about you, your brain and your future.

So it is very much a YOU-centered self-help program.

You. YOu. YOU.

Your brain is going to be your best and closest friend.

Stand by your brain, always, whilst it is thinking.

You are but your brain; your brain is what makes you tick.

But, also please do not forget: **SMILE, SMILE, SMILE.**

Summary: Befriending Your Brain

ॐ You and your brain 'duality' – think in terms of *consciousness/corporeal body* and *your brain* (if that helps).

ॐ The absolute need to wish your brain a *good morning* first thing, each day.

ॐ You and your brain are not strangers.

ॐ Your brain knows you; <u>now</u> you have to get to know your brain better.

ॐ Having a mental image, a metaphor, <u>an icon</u> or 'feeling' to represent your brain

ॐ The befriending and nurturing process gets you in-synch with your brain, achieving the *'oneness'* we seek.

ॐ The befriending/nurturing process consists of 4 mandatory (non-negotiable) daily activities, which are:

> 1. *Good morning* ritual.
>
> 2. Regular, routine brain *pings* – at least 10 a day (while awake).
>
> 3. Maintaining awareness of your brain at all times, throughout the day.
>
> 4. *Good night* ritual

ॐ Befriending activities trigger the brain to release '***happy chemicals***', e.g., **dopamine** & **serotonin**.

ॐ *Day's highlights reel* is not mandatory, but it should help you fall asleep and have sweeter dreams.

ॐ No more references to *willpower'*, instead it will always be *willingness* between you and your brain.

ॐ The 3 'C's of your future relationship with your brain: *cooperation, collaboration* & *camaraderie.*

ॐ ***Thinking about thinking.***

ॐ Going forward your brain will be your closest friend.

 (3 *THINK, THINK, THINK.*

(3 *SMILE, SMILE, SMILE.*

(3 Think about YOU – it is the best form of meditation.

Exercises:

1. Greet your brain with *good morning, good afternoon* or whatever is appropriate.

2. *Ping* your brain.

3. **Think** of your brain.

Rodin Museum, Philadelphia

Keywords & Phrases From 'Befriending Your Brain'

- ✓ *Good morning!*

- ✓ Brain *pings*.

- ✓ Brain/You *duality*.

- ✓ Day's highlights.

- ✓ Befriending.

- ✓ **Dopamine.**

- ✓ Awareness.

- ✓ Willingness.

- ✓ Consciousness.

- ✓ Never an imbalance.

- ✓ Shoulder angels.

- ✓ Will forever change your life.

- ✓ *Mississippi one, Mississippi two.*

- ✓ *Cooperation, collaboration* and *camaraderie*.

- ✓ *"How am **I** doing?"*

- ✓ **THINK.**

- ✓ **SMILE**

4.
BRAIN MEDITATION

'Brain meditation' is based on thinking. It is active meditation on-the-go, throughout the course of the day, via one form of thinking or another.

Mindful thinking is the basis of any form of meditation. 'Brain meditation' sets out to maximize the amount of such thinking, <u>done by you</u>, on a *daily basis*. All of the mindful thinking you do counts as 'brain meditation'. 'Brain meditation', as such, is pure mental meditation. You do not require any pre-allocated, dedicated time for 'brain meditation'. 'Brain meditation' is meant to be done in *timeshare (i.e., background) mode.*

So, the thinking involved in 'brain meditation' should to be done while you are engaged in doing other things, e.g., brushing your teeth, taking a shower, waiting in line, taking a bathroom break, out exercising, sitting at traffic lights, etc. [*You have seen the picture in chapter 2.*]

'Brain meditation' can be done in *quick fire*, short duration bursts. You, however, have to do it as often as possible, on a daily basis. Each 'burst' (or 'session') only has to last a few seconds. But, you need to make sure that you do at least twenty (20) such *'sessions'* a day. As you go along you will find that you will be doing more than that. Why? Because, to put it bluntly, 'brain meditation' is addictive! You will look forward to your *'quick fire'* bursts of meditation. You will find them relaxing. You will find that they are calming. Way down the road you will discover a deep, inner sense of serenity.

The thinking associated with 'brain meditation', though done in *timeshare mode*, will not make you appear distracted or preoccupied. Part of that has to do with its 'quick fire' nature. Another factor is that your *amazing* brain will make sure that you remain attentive to your surroundings while you and your brain do 'brain meditation' in the background.

Something else you should always keep in mind when it comes to this program. Communing with your brain will inevitably result in beneficial increases in the levels of ***dopamine*** and other *feel good* chemicals in your brain. *(You have seen the picture.)* This is not hyperbole, black magic or smoke-and-mirrors. Some forms of meditation, exercise (including yoga) and listening to music are known to stimulate these *feel good* brain chemicals. 'Brain meditation' activities, which involve proactive, positive brain interactions, definitely fall within the category of such trigger mechanisms for dopamine, oxytocin, serotonin, etc.

When To Commence

It is best NOT to start the *befriending/ nurturing* and *'brain meditation'* at the same time.

Start the *befriending* process first. Do those four *befriending* activities, <u>daily</u>, for a couple of weeks (or more) before you start the activities described in this chapter.

So, ideally it is a staggered start: *befriending*, on its own, for a few weeks before starting the *mindful thinking* processes described in this chapter.

The need for this staggered start, however, is not chiseled in stone.

The staggered start is just to give you an opportunity to get the befriending protocols firmly entrenched in your system without the additional distractions of <u>virtualization/mindful thinking</u>. But, it is your call, entirely. If you feel you can bypass the initial 'acclimatization' phase, please go ahead and start the 'Full Monty' at the same time, or with a shorter interval. OK? Your decision.

The Crux Of 'Brain Meditation'

There are <u>two forms</u> of mindful thinking used to achieve 'brain meditation':

1. *Virtualization* – which can also be thought of and referred to as *visualization*. [Virtualization = Visualization]

2. Everyday thinking, but in particular *'thinking for pleasure'*.

Virtualization – Meditation Via Thinking Ahead

Virtualization is about proactively thinking about your future.

Virtualization is about anticipating the future. It is about projecting yourself, as *realistically as possible*, into future situations. You can even think of it as productive daydreaming, albeit with intent, direction and purpose.

> *Virtualization makes you think.*

It makes you think about your future. The process of thinking focuses your brain – grounds it, centers it and calms it. Hence, why virtualization is at the core of 'brain meditation'.

Virtualization is meant to be done in timeshare mode – e.g., when brushing your teeth or taking a shower.

I prefer to call it virtualization rather than **'visualization'** because there is a subtle difference.

Virtualization is always about your *hoped-for reality* or your *anticipated reality*. With virtualization we can only <u>hope</u>. There is no guarantee that the future will pan out exactly as we had hoped. Hence my desire to capture that with the notion of 'virtual'. But, feel free to use 'visualization' if that sits better with you. OK?

Virtualization is by no means a technique specific to 'brain meditation'. Far from it. Virtualization has been widely and very successfully used in the world of sports for decades (if not longer). It has been proven to be exceptionally effective in sports that involve some kind of pre-set course or routine; e.g., motor racing, skiing, speed skating, track events, marathons, gymnastics, bike racing, competitive sailing, cross-country, figure skating, horse racing, etc.

With sports-related virtualization you 'run' the course, track or routine, in its entirety, in your head. You, however, in reality, will be standing still, sitting or maybe even lying down. But, in your mind's eye, you are busily weaving through the course (or routine), doing complex physical feats, at the optimum speed that they are supposed to be performed. You actually see, in your mind, all the actions and maneuvers that you need to perform in order to succeed. You react to them in your mind. You live the event, in your mind, multiple times (if necessary) prior to doing it for real. That is virtualization as it pertains to sports.

Virtualization within the realm of 'brain meditation' is no different. It is about looking ahead to what lies ahead and how you should plan for it.

Virtualization, as with most things 'brain meditation', is about YOU and YOU ALONE.

Virtualization is divided into four different kinds (or classes) based on the **timeframes** involved. So, the four different kinds are:

1. **Short-term**: thinking ahead, a *few minutes* into the future, possibly up to *6 hours away*.

2. **Mid-term**: thinking ahead to later the *same day* – and up to 3 days away.

3. **Long-term**: thinking ahead, starting 3 to 4 days from 'now' and extending out a week or two.

4. **Blue-Sky**: thinking ahead, somewhere out there in the future, maybe six months out, maybe a year and possibly even further out (though ideally less than 5 years away).

Short-term & Mid-term virtualization is mandatory to this program. That is your primary form of 'brain meditation'.

All four forms of virtualization are always done in 'Fast Forward (FF)' (expedited time), in timeshare mode, e.g., brushing teeth, taking a shower, or waiting to get a cup of coffee.

Virtualization focuses your mind.

Virtualization brings focus to your life.

You will find, with time, that virtualization is *soothing* – leading towards that sought-after *serenity*. There are two (2) aspects to this soothing:

a. Focusing the brain and pushing out distractions, i.e., our 'brain meditation', is soothing in its own right. It is meant to be as such. Virtualization also precludes your brain from wondering. If you have tendencies towards nervousness or anxiety the act of virtualization serves as a very effective counter.

b. That you are planning for the future will, moreover, prove to be soothing and calm inducing. It is preparing you for what is to come. To a degree it is all about: *forewarned is forearmed*. It provides you with a sense of *déjà vu* for the future! Virtualization gives you a chance to look into the future.

Long-term and Blue-Sky virtualizations are not mandatory to this program. Ideally, in time, it would be good if you did all four forms. But, to begin with it is acceptable if you restrict your efforts to short- and mid-term. In general, most people tend to focus upon, enjoy, and get the most benefit from short-term virtualizations. And, that is fine. Start with that.

Short-term Virtualization: The Specifics

A short-term virtualization, <u>*daily*</u>, while getting started for the day ahead, is a must. This is meant to be done while getting ready for the day, i.e., brushing your teeth, taking a shower, styling your hair, getting dressed, etc. During this virtualization you think of what lies ahead of <u>*you*</u> for the day. You know, at a minimum, in rough terms (broad brush), what the day is supposed to hold for you; what things you are supposed to be doing, where you are supposed to be, etc.

So, think ahead. Start living your day, in your mind, ahead of what is to unfold.

> Get a jumpstart on your day, in your mind
> – through virtualization.

I know that you understand what I am getting at. Virtualization is not difficult to grasp.

You should incorporate **some role-play** into your virtualizations. Visualize others and how they will influence your day – your future. Role-play these interactions. Virtualize both sides of the interactions.

You do not stop what you are doing to virtualize. That is not how it works. You virtualize while doing routine tasks during the course of the day.

With short-term virtualization you look ahead a couple of hours. You try to anticipate what will transpire during that time period. You come up with a 'plan' as to how you would like things to proceed. Of course, you will have to make adjustments since real life will never go exactly according to your hopes. There is that famous saying that *'the best laid plans of mice and men often go awry'*.

In your first virtualization of the day you come up with an overall 'plan' for <u>that day</u>. Then during the course of the day you refine that 'plan'. You get more specific as the 'window' that you are looking ahead at becomes narrower.

After your initial virtualization it might be 30 to 90 minutes before you get a chance to do another. It is best, however, to keep the interval between virtualizations as short as possible. Remember that short-term virtualizations are not meant to take long. Two-seconds, max, at a time. *Mississippi One, Mississippi Two* … and you are done.

So, following the first, your <u>next</u> short-term virtualization maybe while you are: getting some breakfast, standing in line for a cup of coffee, sitting at traffic lights (or just plain traffic), or whatever. It will depend on your life, your schedule. But, you get the drift. *It is an iterative, one-after-the-other, process.* One quick short-term virtualization and then another, ideally within two-hours. Each time you look ahead a few hours into the future. You plan for the next few hours. You anticipate the next few hours.

You keep on kicking the short-term virtualization 'can' down the road -- till you reach the end of your day.

OK? Virtualization is NOT a difficult concept to grasp, master or practice. It is very intuitive. It is very helpful. Very relaxing.

<u>*Why Virtualize?*</u>

Virtualization is the primary basis of 'brain meditation'.

Virtualization is a powerful mechanism by which to commune with your brain. It is how you can spend some quality time with your brain on a regular basis, throughout the day.

Virtualization is how we proactively engage our brain into helping us navigate life on an ongoing basis. This routine (ritualistic) virtualization creates a strong bond between you and your brain.

So, a very good reason to virtualize, and virtualize often, is that it gets you to spend matchless quality time with your brain.

With virtualization you are trying, always, to see if you can *steal a march* on your future. You are striving to gain an advantage, an edge – be it, however small. You are setting out to be better prepared. Trying to gainfully anticipate what may be around the next corner without spending any dedicated time trying to do so *per se.*

> ➤ **It is all about being *forewarned* to be better *forearmed.*** ◁

Virtualization will *soothe* you at two different *levels*, and at two different *times*.

Virtualization by itself is soothing (even though you will be doing it in timeshare mode). It focuses your brain. It centers your brain. *It also stimulates all those 'happy' brain chemicals.* So, that is the first level of soothing – as well as the first instance of soothing.

The next level/next time of soothing will occur down the road. At some point you will actually come face to face with a scenario that you had already 'virtualized' beforehand. *BINGO!* That is when you will notice a *second level* of soothing. Why? Because you feel, to your relief, that you have already been here, *already done that!* A kind of *déjà vu.*

Virtualization is in essence a way of rehearsing for *your* future. Going through the motions ahead of time in *your* mind. It helps you to be better prepared – for *your* future.

The more you virtualize the better you will become at anticipating different outcomes. You will start to formulate **contingency plans**. Further down the road you will start creating contingency plans for your contingency plans! This is all good. Anticipating the future, realistically, is never a bad thing.

Is Virtualization A Waste Of Time?

You could rephrase that and ask: *'is trying to be better prepared for what the future may hold a waste of time'*?

But, even leaving that aside, what 'time' are you wasting with virtualization? Virtualization is always done in timeshare (background) mode. You virtualize while making a cup of coffee, buttering the toast, flossing your teeth, pounding a treadmill …

Now you can go ahead and answer the 'waste of time' question on your own.

Is There Any Danger In Virtualizing?

Yes, there is a chance that virtualizing in timeshare mode could be a distraction. You may spill the coffee or put hair gel on your toothbrush rather than toothpaste. Yes, it could happen – especially in the early days.

But as you persevere, as I hope you will, you should discover that your brain will allow you to virtualize without it being too distracting. Your brain typically has more than enough processing power to deftly cope with significant amounts of multitasking. So, it will let you virtualize without spilling the coffee. You will become attuned to virtualizing in background mode without it getting in the way of your ongoing daily life.

Longer term Virtualizations

Mid-term virtualizations should take a little longer than the typical two-seconds spent on short-term virtualizations. That is due to you trying to cover a longer timeframe. But, even then, you might not have to devote more than a few minutes, per virtualization – and that, yet again, in timeshare mode. When exercising, e.g., walking, jogging, swimming, or cycling, is a great time to practice longer term virtualizations. Other excellent opportunities for thinking ahead include: sitting in a waiting room, getting your teeth cleaned, or being a passenger in any kind of vehicle, whether it be a bus, car, plane, train, ferry, monorail, or rickshaw.

> *Don't be bored; virtualize instead.*

You will be surprised as to how much ground you can cover in a couple of minutes – once you get immersed in this program.

If it helps think of these longer-term virtualizations as *focused daydreaming*. Daydreaming with a definite purpose. Rather than letting your mind wonder (aimlessly) do some blue-sky virtualization. That is not to say that you cannot, henceforth, ever let your mind wonder, or daydream outside of virtualization. Yes, you can do those things too, provided, of course, that you allocate adequate time for virtualization. *Moderation.* Moderation in everything. Allocate time slots for all the things you want to do. Allocate some time for daydreaming, and some for virtualization. Moderation. Balance. Compromise. Discipline. All good things, that will stand you in good stead.

Two Virtualization Exercises

1. Virtualizing a **trip** that you intend to make.

2. Virtualizing a doctor/dentist/therapist/nurse **appointment**.

Virtualizing **a trip**: The destination of this trip is a place, a distance away, that you need to visit. You are either going to drive/ride/cycle there or take public transport. If you have previously been there you would have some idea as to what the trip involves. If you are, however, not familiar with how to get there you should do some research as to what the trip would entail. Either way you should try virtualizing *the* trip when you have the time.

Get as detailed and specific as you can. Try and visualize each and every aspect, diligently. Virtualize all the steps involved. What needs to be done, and when. Actions that will be expected of you. What things you will need, e.g., toll money, tickets, identification, etc. Travel the entire trip, in minute detail, in your mind. Live it in your mind's eye. Be like the downhill skier virtualizing the course ahead of the race. Virtualize the trip, from start to finish.

Virtualizing an **appointment**: Yet again the goal is to be as precise and realistic as possible. Start with being in the waiting room or even with arriving at the facility. Include role-play. Imagine dialogues. Hear, in your mind, your name being called. Go through your expectations and/or concerns. Anticipate different scenarios, both positive and those that are not as positive. As with the trip scenario above, live through the entire appointment, visualizing as much of the likely interactions, with as much detail as you can muster.

Virtualization exercises like these are extremely beneficial ahead of a real trip or an appointment. They prepare you for what could lie ahead. You would have minimized some of the potential surprises. You would be better forearmed. You will, as such, be able to be more relaxed during the trip or appointment. Experience that *déjà vu feeling*. Things will never go exactly as you imagined. The virtualization, however, would have established some degree of familiarity with what is to come. And that, come the time, will stand you in good stead. Being forewarned so that you can be forearmed for the future.

Bolstering Virtualization With 'Everyday Thinking'

All mindful thinking counts as 'brain meditation'.

Virtualization is the 'brain meditation' specific form of mindful thinking. Other forms of mindful thinking performed during the course of a day will also help the 'brain meditation' cause. This is particularly the case with mindful thinking for pleasure.

The various forms of thinking that you can indulge in are covered in *the next chapter*.

Any and all thinking, particularly when done *mindfully* (i.e., with an awareness that your brain is engaged in thinking), keeps your brain focused and centered. Typically a thinking brain tends to be calmer – even if dealing with problems and strife. It all has to do with the brain being focused. The brain, therefore, is less prone to gravitate towards thought processes that cause agitation. Furthermore, a befriended brain, conditioned via daily 'brain meditation', when involved in mindful thinking will be more attune to being calm and grounded.

The bottom line here is that while daily virtualization is a non-negotiable must for 'brain meditation', all of the other mindful thinking you do also count as part of your 'brain meditation' effort. It adds to the quota of time spent a day in gainful 'brain meditation'.

When You Will Start Seeing The Rewards Of 'brain meditation'

You will not detect any results for at least 4 months.

'Brain meditation' is a cumulative process. You have to do the prescribed activities (e.g., morning ritual, virtualization, etc.) daily and diligently for *some months* before you start to see the initial changes to your being.

This is not a self-help program that delivers instant gratification. Far from it. You are unlikely to see any changes in the short-term. It will be at least four months, probably closer to six, before you slowly start to detect that you have begun to change. At that stage you would have started to become a 'thinking person' – the new 'Thinking You'.

So please be patient. 'Brain meditation' will change your life for the better – but it cannot do so overnight. Just stick with it. The changes will occur. It is inevitable. 'Brain meditation' on a daily basis will always work – within a few months. It has to. It is like faithfully sticking to a meaningful diet or exercise regimen. *The results will follow* The process has to work. The effort you put in does not just dissipate into thin air. *It does condition the brain.*

'Brain meditation', as you have already seen, is not onerous. There is nothing complicated or strenuous. It demands very little from you. You can do it in timeshare mode and there are no costs associated with it. Just embrace the program with passion and wait for the rewards to kick in. {SMILE}

Summary: Brain Meditation

ଔ *Thinking*, but specifically *mindful thinking*, performed routinely during the course of a day is the basis for 'brain meditation'.

ଔ Any and all *mindful thinking* counts as 'brain meditation'.

ଔ 'Brain meditation', in particular the virtualizations, can be done in *quick fire, timeshare mode* – albeit multiple times a day, as often as possible (with 6 times/day a bare minimum).

ଔ Ideally you will start the 'brain meditation' activities two- to four-weeks after starting the *'befriending the brain'* process.

ଔ The mindful thinking involved in 'brain meditation' consists of:
1/ *virtualization/visualization* & **2/** everyday thinking.

ଔ Virtualization is about you proactively thinking about/*anticipating* your future as a means of focusing, centering and calming your brain.

ଔ There are four (4) different forms of virtualizations based on the timeframes involved.
They are: 1/ **short-term**, 2/ **mid-term**, 3/ **long-term** & 4/ **blue-sky**.

ଔ *Short-term & mid-term virtualization is mandatory.*

ଔ Virtualization is soothing at multiple levels; doing it calms you, and *down the road* it helps you, via a kind of *déjà vu*, to better confront life as it unfolds -- with *equanimity* and aplomb.

ଔ Daily, while getting *started for the day* (e.g., brushing teeth) you get into your 'brain meditation' routine by doing a short-term virtualization that looks ahead at that day.

ଔ You do additional virtualizations as the day progresses, each time kicking the can forward a few hours into the future.

ଔ A short-term virtualization covering 3 to 4 hours into the future can be done in two-seconds, within the brain, in fast forward (FF) mode.

ଔ Virtualize whenever you get a chance – throughout your day.

ଔ Virtualization is fun and can become addictive in a very good way.

Exercises:

1. Virtualizing a trip that you plan to make.

2. *Virtualizing* an appointment with a caregiver (e.g., doctor or therapist).

Northern New Hampshire

Keywords & Phrases From 'Brain Meditation'

- ✓ Mindful thinking.

- ✓ Pure mental meditation.

- ✓ Everyday thinking.

- ✓ *Virtualization = Visualization.*

- ✓ Hoped for reality/anticipated reality.

- ✓ *Forewarned is forearmed.*

- ✓ A sense of *déjà vu.*

- ✓ Short-term virtualization.

- ✓ Don't be bored, virtualize instead.

- ✓ Focused daydreaming.

- ✓ Fast forward mode.

- ✓ Role playing.

- ✓ All thinking counts.

- ✓ Contingency plans.

- ✓ It has to work!

- ✓ Blue-sky.

- ✓ Daily and diligence.

- ✓ Patience.

- ✓ *Thinking You.*

- ✓ **SMILE.**

5.
VARIOUS FORMS
OF THINKING

Thinking can, and should, be an exquisite pleasure.

There is much to be said for thinking for the sake of thinking.

Mindful thinking is having an *awareness* within yourself that you are involved in the process of thinking. In other words, being *conscious* that you are engaged in thinking (as opposed to thinking being just a 'blur').

Everyday thinking, when done mindfully, is a form of 'brain meditation'. As such it counts towards your daily quota of time spent doing 'brain meditation'.

Too many folks delude themselves into believing that they are either too busy to think, or that they do not have anything worthwhile to think about. Both are patently false.

The following four (4) statements about 'thinking' are demonstrably true and you should take heed of them.

1. Irrespective of what your life (or lifestyle) is, you will never have a shortage of things that you can gainfully think about, *every day*, for the rest of your life.

2. Irrespective of how busy you believe yourself to be, you will always have time, **every day**, for some amount of thinking – just for the incomparable pleasure of thinking.

3. Irrespective of what you have previously thought, thinking does not have to be a chore and, with practice, you will find it to be a very *pleasurable endeavor*.

4. Irrespective of your current emotional/mental state, daily thinking, as a *form of meditation*, will slowly introduce a degree of calmness into your life which will, over time, evolve into a sense of *serenity*.

Some Things To Think About 'Thinking'

o You can always find time to think. If nothing else, think 'bathroom breaks'. But, if you think about it, all lives have many natural breaks during the day, whether it be: to get a drink, grab a snack or to change clothes. To begin with you just need to think about thinking whenever you have such a quick break.

o No one's life is too mundane to warrant not having anything worthwhile to think about – *for the sheer pleasure of thinking.*

o Unless you are comatose you can't go through a single day without doing some amount of thinking. It might be very humdrum along the lines of: *'what shall I eat?'* or *'should I eat this?'* You have to make some decisions every day, however basic they may be, just to get through life. And you can't make decisions without some modicum of thought. Think of it as *'thinking to survive'* (or *'survival thinking'*).

o Being physically busy (e.g., travelling or attending meetings) does not mean that your brain doesn't have any time to think. Do not confuse frenetic physical activity with actually being too busy to think.

o Build a library of *'Comfort Thoughts'* that you can seek shelter in whenever you feel stressed – even if that stress is caused by the requirement to do virtualizations or every day thinking! {SMILE}

o Thinking, *personal thinking* in particular, is a very effective means of *relaxation*; a form of personal *escapism*.

o Use personal thinking to rationalize, compartmentalize and come-to-terms-with the problems that bother you.

o Think for the sake of thinking. Think for the sheer pleasure of thinking. Revel in the process and pleasure of thinking.

> *"Think left and think right and think low and think high.*
> *Oh, the thinks you can think up if only you try!"*

> -- Theodor Seuss Geisel (i.e., Dr. Seuss)

<u>*Can Never Be A Shortage Of Things To Think About*</u>

There is really no end of *'thinks'* to think about if you will only get around to thinking about them!

Just a small sampling of stuff you could think about would include: names, numbers, time, colors, plants, animals, religion, the Universe, people, places, history, books, music, flight, great artists, politicians, life, meaning of life, volcanoes, mystics, movies, the after-life, Dr. Seuss, yourself, your dreams, your achievements, etc., etc.

There is no end of *'thinks'* you can think about.

You just have to make a habit of thinking about things – something, anything and everything.

<u>*Different Types Of Thinking*</u>

In terms of this program 'thinking' can be divided into seven (7) different types (or forms), with 'personal thinking' capable of being divided into four (4) sub-categories. So 'thinking' can be categorized as follows:

1. Thinking in order to get by in your day-to-day life.

2. Thinking for solving problems.

3. Thinking in order to make major decisions.

4. Thinking so as to learn things.

5. *Virtualization.*

6. Personal Thinking –

   - for pleasure.

   - for knowledge and edification.

   - for relaxation and serenity.

   - for minimizing and *containing* worry.

7. Thinking in your sleep.

<u>*Few Notes On The Different Types Of Thinking*</u>

☼ The above 7-type categorization is just meant to serve as a 'map' to provoke thought – within the context of this program. You could come up with different categorizations, equally valid, and there will invariably be some overlap among the categories – yours or those listed above.

✿ *'Thinking for problem solving'* is what many people associate with thinking. That is mainly because they have never given any real thought to what they think about! This type of thinking should not be the primary way we utilize our brain. Luckily for us we can't get through life without doing other types of thinking.

✿ As long as we are conscious, we have to do some amount of thinking -- *survival thinking* -- on a daily ongoing basis, in order to just *'keep our head above water'*. This is independent of the life-sustaining *'autonomic functions'* performed by your brain, in conjunction with your nervous system. These include everything from regulating heart rate to digestion, not to mention sneezing, coughing, urination and sexual arousal.

✿ Our daily virtualizations should try to include some 'survival' eventualities – especially those having to do with sustenance (e.g., *'what shall I have for breakfast?'*), grooming (e.g., *'do I really need to take a shower?'*) and your day's schedule (e.g., *'how long is it going to take me to get to that appointment if the traffic is going to be crazy?'*). Also, factor in contingencies.

✿ This 'brain meditation' program will make you more *decisive*; you will make decisions faster and you will learn not to second-guess them. You will become more confident and fluent at making decisions, big or small.

✿ There is a big difference, in the thought processes involved, between making *workaday/survival* decisions and those that are more 'major' and possibly life altering; e.g., the difference between *'what shall I have for breakfast?'* and *'should I start looking for a new job?'*, or between *'what shall I wear today?'* and *'am I ready to propose marriage?'* So, that is the distinction between #1 & #3 in the above 7-item list.

✿ *Thinking for problem solving* does not always have to be about complex issues. It could just be one level up from *survival thinking*, e.g., *'what is the channel number for the local weather?'*, *'how much should I pay on each of my credit card balances?'*, or *'do I have enough gas to get to my usual gas station or should I stop and get gas now?'*

Personal Thinking To Contain Worry (And Help Relaxation)

Personal thinking (sometimes with virtualization) should help you better cope with your problems and worries. Though it might not be a complete cure it should enable you to formulate ways to contain your worries. *Personal thinking*/virtualization will enable you to better deal, *emotionally*, with what you have to contend with.

o   *Personal thinking* should be used (relentlessly if need be) to enable you to rationalize and better understand what causes you to worry. *This rationalization is important and the key to any type of worry containment.* Working with your brain, keep on going over and over the sources of worry so as to appreciate which aspects cause what types of anxiety/stress.

o   Learn to *compartmentalize* the causes of worry; i.e., breaking down the causes/problems into smaller and smaller sub-components. Then determine which of these sub-components you might be able to better tackle, and with luck contain (or possibly even dismiss). Google *'problem compartmentalization'* techniques.

o   Ask your brain to help you *'come to terms'* with some aspects of your worries. Relate it to the you-brain *willingness* notion that was talked about in the *'befriending the brain'* chapter (i.e., chapter 3).

o   Try to use *thinking for pleasure*, *problem solving thinking* or *virtualization* to keep your mind busy and prevent it from gravitating towards 'worry'.

o   Discuss with your brain (in earnest) as to the worries that bother you. Ask your brain what steps you can take together (leveraging the techniques mentioned above) to contain the worries.

o   *Worry is just another manifestation of your brain at work!* Worry, if you think about it, is just another form of thinking (somewhere between 'survival thinking' and 'problem solving thinking') – a negative, extreme and dark form be it. Like pain, it is all in your brain. But, just like pain it does have a purpose. It is a warning light of sorts. The *key*, however, is that it is all in your brain. That means that you should be able to, with the help of your brain, keep it within bounds. Try to keep it in check. It will need work. It will not be easy – at first. It is, nonetheless, something well worth working towards utilizing the protocols/disciplines of 'brain meditation'.

Thinking In Your Sleep: Parameters

o *Thinking in your sleep* is very different to thinking while you are trying to get to sleep; i.e., one is *pre-sleep thinking* while the other is *thinking while asleep*.

o *Thinking in your sleep* is not a far-fetched, pie-in-the-sky, 'looney tunes', new-age 'mumbo-jumbo'. Quite a few people already do this – they just don't talk about it. Maybe you are one of them.

o *Thinking in your sleep* is not necessarily the same as *'let me sleep on that'*. The latter typically is just an indication of wanting more time to think about an issue rather than thinking about that issue while sleeping *per se*.

o *Thinking in your sleep* (a.k.a. *sleep thinking*) is an *optional*, value-add to 'brain meditation'. As such not doing it will not impact the rest of your 'brain meditation' regimen or rewards.

o Do not attempt to *sleep think* if you are having issues sleeping. Sleeping well, i.e., getting a good "night's" sleep (or a good day's sleep if your days are reversed), is much more important than *sleep thinking*. First let 'brain meditation' help you sleep better before you contemplate trying *sleep thinking*.

o *Sleep thinking* is easy to master and you should be able to try it out within a month of starting 'brain meditation'.

o *Sleep thinking* works best when you have a *specific 'problem'* or 'issue' to deal with; e.g., determining the pros and cons of two options, figuring out ways to overcome a challenge, working out the best way to do something or making choices between alternatives. It is most effective when it involves *decision making* – when there is a *definable outcome* at stake.

o *Sleep thinking* can be a very effective means of validating buying decisions. It also works well in helping you prioritize options.

o *Sleep thinking* works best when you can provide your brain with *lots of data* that *'it'* can process – on your behalf, while you sleep. It does not work as well when you cannot provide your brain with sufficient information. This is because *sleep thinking* is all about crunching existing data while you sleep.

o *Sleep thinking* can be very *rewarding* and *fulfilling*. There can be a *'magical'* and *'mystical'* element to it. When done successfully (which could become the norm), there is inevitably a sense of accomplishment.

Sleep Thinking: The Mechanics

➤ If you intend to *sleep think* you first need to *complete* your 'good night' ritual before you begin preparing yourself for *sleep thinking*.

➤ Following your 'good night' ritual you should drift into your *ready-to-fall-asleep* mode. Your eyes will be closed. You would turn off/dim the lights per your usual routine. There should be no distractions to interfere with sleep. You should be physically comfortable and at ease; breathing normally.

➤ *Sleep thinking* involves a 5-step process:

1. Formulating the 'issue' with as much specificity as you can.

2. Handing over the 'issue' to your brain.

3. Giving your brain time to work on the 'issue'.

4. Obtaining the 'output' of the *sleep thinking* from your brain upon awakening.

5. Making decisions if applicable, when awake, based on what was determined via *sleep thinking*.

➤ Clearly formulating the 'issue': You do this by *bringing it to mind* (so to speak). Ponder on it, slowly, eyes closed. *Virtualize* the issue. Ensure that your brain has a very clear picture of what you want it to think about while you sleep.

➤ Handing over the 'issue' to your brain: First you have to be sure that you have done a good job defining the 'issue' to your brain. Once you are happy with that you need to make a deliberate 'gesture' of handing over the issue to your brain. You can even tell your brain: *"OK? That is the 'issue'. Over to you. You work on it and let me know in the morning. Thanks, much. Good night. Sweet dreams."* Ideally try and get some kind of acknowledgement from your brain. Then let the brain work on the 'issue'. Try and drift off to sleep.

➤ It might be some time before the brain gets around to doing the *sleep thinking*. There are certain *housekeeping* tasks that might have priority, e.g., cataloging the day's memories or cueing up your dream sequences for the night. Your brain, however, can, and will, multitask when it has to. So, some activities will take place in parallel as you sleep. As such, *sleep thinking* should not preclude you from having dreams. Some dreams may incorporate elements from the 'issue' being pondered. That is a bonus.

➤ How you obtain the results from your *sleep thinking* may vary. In some instances the brain will start presenting you with the 'output', unasked. You will have a distinct awareness of the results the brain wants you to know about. In other instances you may have to ask the brain as to what conclusions it reached. The urgency/magnitude of the 'issue' is sometimes a determining factor here, i.e., as to whether you have to ask or whether the brain will start sharing as soon as you are awake.

➤ You will get better at *sleep thinking* with practice. You can 'sleep think' the same 'issue' multiple nights. Do not get discouraged at the start. Persevere.

Summary: Various Forms Of Thinking

ᘓ You can always find time to think, and there is never a shortage of things to think about.

ᘓ Thinking should never be a chore.

ᘓ Daily thinking, provided it is *mindful*, is always a form of 'brain meditation'.

ᘓ Do not equate being physically busy with your brain not having any time to think.

ᘓ Build up a library of *comfort thoughts* that you can turn to, whenever, for solace.

ᘓ There are seven (7) different types of thinking:
1/ **'survival' (get by) thinking**, 2/ **problem solving thinking**,
3/ **decision making thinking**, 4/ **thinking to learn**, 5/ **virtualization**,
6/ **personal thinking** & 7/ **sleep thinking**.

ᘓ 'Personal thinking' can be divided into that what we do for:
1/ pleasure, **2/** knowledge & edification, **3/** relaxation & serenity &
4/ minimizing and containing worry.

ᘓ *There is more to thinking than just problem solving.*

ᘓ 'Brain meditation' will make you more decisive and better able to deal with, composure, the decisions you make.

ᘓ Worry is but a variation of thinking, and as such other forms of thinking can be used to contain that worry.

ᘓ Understanding what causes worry is the first step in being able to contain that worry.

ᘓ *Sleep thinking*, though optional, is an easy to master, and very useful, technique.

ᘓ *Sleep thinking* is most effective when there is specificity to the issue and when you can provide your brain with lots of data to process.

೮ There is a five (5) step process to *sleep thinking*:

    1/ formulating the issue,

    2/ handing the issue over to the brain,

    3/ giving the brain time to think while you sleep,

    4/ obtaining the 'output'/results from the brain &

    5/ making the relevant decisions, once awake, based on 'output'/results.

Fall in Central New Hampshire

Keywords & Phrases From 'Various Forms Of Thinking'

- ✓ *Thinking for the sake of thinking.*

- ✓ Being *aware* that you are thinking.

- ✓ No life is too mundane to preclude thinking.

- ✓ Bathroom breaks = time to think.

- ✓ Personal thinking = relaxation.

- ✓ Library of *comfort thoughts.*

- ✓ Containing worry.

- ✓ Worry is but another variation of thinking!

- ✓ *Compartmentalization.*

- ✓ Coping.

- ✓ Composure.

- ✓ *Sleep thinking* is optional.

- ✓ *Sleep thinking* is easy to master.

- ✓ Crunching existing data.

- ✓ Autonomic functions.

- ✓ Dr. Seuss!

- ✓ Thinking should be an exquisite pleasure.

- ✓ **Smile.**

- ✓ **Think.**

6.

POWER THINKING

Practicing 'brain meditation' conditions you and your brain to better utilize the *inborn power* and capacity of your brain.

Daily 'brain meditation' <u>fine-tunes</u> your brain to ensure that it can work more efficiently than before. 'Brain meditation' **does not** increase the IQ you were born with. It, however, helps you use more of your brain, with more vigor and precision, than what you were previously capable.

To use the earlier analogy (from chapter 2), if your brain is an engine, 'brain meditation' does not set out to provide you with a bigger or more powerful engine. Instead, it makes sure that the engine you already possess is capable, in terms of the adjustments and tuning it needs, to run as close to its peak efficiency.

'Brain meditation', as you now know, increases the intimacy and intensity of the relationship between you and your (better attuned) brain. This enhanced relationship coupled with the extra processing capacity unleashed in your brain, gives you the *option* of indulging in some *power thinking* techniques.

There are three techniques that you may want to consider. They are:

1. **Accelerated Thinking**

2. **Background Thinking**

3. **Parallel Thinking**

As with *sleep thinking* (in chapter 5), all three of these 'power thinking' techniques are not essential for practicing 'brain meditation', i.e., they are *optional*. They are value-added *benefits* arising from 'brain meditation'. You can decide to skip any or all of them without in any way compromising your commitment to 'brain meditation'. Each is independent in its own right, though one has to acknowledge that there is some commonality between *sleep thinking*, *background thinking* and *parallel thinking*.

Only consider learning <u>one or more</u> of these techniques if you feel that they could be of **benefit** to you. That said, 'accelerated thinking' is definitely worth exploring.

If you master *sleep thinking* (the easiest of all the techniques), you will be at least 70% along the way towards acing *background thinking*. As such, it would be a shame not to give *background thinking* a try.

Parallel thinking, on the other hand, is a bit complicated and hard. It is best left till last. If you find that *sleep thinking* and *background thinking* are 'a breeze' and rewarding, then you might want to, as well, try out *parallel thinking*.

Accelerated Thinking

Accelerated thinking is the ability to *up shift, on demand,* the speed and intensity of your thinking.

It is the *skill* of being able to ask your brain to *think faster* and actually *feel your brain respond*! It will feel like putting your foot down, hard, on the accelerator pedal of a very powerful sports car and then feeling it respond, eagerly, to that *kick down*. In the beginning you may actually perceive, in your mind, a 'click' and then a surge of energy as your brain lunges into 'accelerated thinking'. *That is your brain's chemicals kicking-in*!

Accelerated thinking is **not** about increasing your inborn IQ. It is to do with asking your brain to function at a *higher level* within its performance spectrum – albeit for a limited period of time.

Accelerated thinking is a burst of peak, or at least near peak, brain-performance – *typically to get you out of an unexpected jam*.

Accelerated thinking is makes your brain sprint (for a short burst of time). Sprinting is facilitated by fitness. And that is where 'brain meditation' comes in. Daily 'brain meditation' conditions the brain for the occasional sprint – i.e., *accelerated thinking*.

Accelerated thinking is *not* an illusion. It is *not* smoke-and-mirrors; pie-in-the-sky. It is a real, palpable phenomenon – that you will be able to feel.

Accelerated thinking is akin to the body's **fight-or-flight** response. Except now we are making it into a *response by the brain* – to help get us out of *jams* through *mental agility*.

Yes, there are indeed *brain chemicals involved.* With *accelerated thinking* we are causing brain chemicals to get activated to give us a burst of enhanced brain power. Simple as that. *"Elementary, my dear Watson,"* as Sherlock Holmes, who would have understood this stuff, would have said.

Invoking 'Accelerated Thinking'

Accelerated thinking, in practice, is only effective when there is a genuine need for it. It does not work too well if there isn't a major enough 'issue' for your brain to truly tuck into. So, it is not something that you should *cry wolf* with.

What would, as such, be a good situation for invoking *accelerated thinking?* It could be when you are attending an important meeting. You get called upon, unexpectedly, to speak. Another situation might be a social gathering, such as a party or a dinner. You, suddenly, to your horror, need to come up with a name, a place, a date, or even worse an excuse/diversion to avoid an embarrassment/'a scene'. *Accelerated thinking,* of course, can also come in handy in exam/test scenarios.

Accelerated thinking should typically be used in moderation (even in exam/test scenarios). It works best when used in short, sharp bursts. It is not meant to be used over extended periods of time. It is like sprinting. However fit you may be, you can't sprint forever. You have to slow down. Ditto when it comes to *accelerated thinking*

You invoke *accelerated thinking* using a trigger word or phrase.

Think is a good and apropos trigger word. *'Think faster',* *'think, think, think',* *'think hard'* or *"let's go"* would also work. Any phrase, impromptu may it be, will, however, also work.

The trigger word/phrase is just an external, artificial *prop.* In practice your desire for your brain to enter *accelerated thinking* is perceived by the brain telepathically (so to speak). *Remember it is all taking place within your brain.* {SMILE} The trigger word/phrase is just a way to verbalize it within your mind.

The trigger word/phrase does not have to be said out loud. You say it to your brain in the same manner as you do your *good morning, good night* and the regular *'hi, how goes it'.*

With practice some people may find that they can invoke *accelerated thinking* without using a word/phrase *per se.* You would get the process going – i.e., get the brain chemicals flowing -- just by thinking of the need to invoke *accelerated thinking.*

Many of you may find that you need to have been faithfully *'brain meditating'* for a few months (or more) before you are able to invoke *accelerated thinking*. You need to have 'conditioned' your brain through the *'brain meditation'* rituals. Otherwise, the brain will not truly respond, in the hoped-for manner, to *accelerated thinking*.

Typically, when you first start invoking *accelerated thinking* you should feel your brain kicking-in. You should feel a surge. That is your brain chemicals doing their thing. Think 'adrenaline'. But, in this instance we are not interested in chemicals/hormones that stimulate your muscles. Instead, we are now dealing with chemicals and electrical impulses, up there, in your brain -- spurring your brain to help *you* think faster, clearer and in more depth.

All this said, there is no guarantee that *accelerated thinking* will *always* deliver. Sometimes the answers you seek may still be outside your reach -- even with your brain in overdrive. Even with *accelerated thinking* your brain can only process information that it posessess or is capable of accessing. So, do not always expect miracles. *Fight or flight* will not always save your bacon; a bull may still outrun you in a field. {SMILE} Ditto for *accelerated thinking*. {SMILE}

Background Thinking

Background thinking and *sleep thinking* are, in essence, two sides of the same coin. *Background thinking* is essentially *sleep thinking* done while awake!

The big difference between the two being the amount of other thinking, in particular *foreground* (i.e., conscious or deliberate) thinking, taking place. During *sleep thinking* your other thinking is at a minimum. During *background thinking* you have to contend with, and make allowances for, other thinking that (most likely) is also taking place.

Background thinking is not meant to be a short-duration activity. For *background thinking* to be effective you need to have periods of *quiet time* during which your brain can do the expected processing. 'Quiet time' in this context are periods where your brain does not have to be on full alert. Examples of such 'quiet time' would be when you are: walking, a passenger in a vehicle, taking a bath, exercising, sitting in a waiting room, eating a meal on your own or pursuing a hobby such as gardening.

So, you can indulge in *background thinking* whenever you are involved in an activity that does not require that much *foreground* thinking on your part. [As such, *some folks* may be able to do some *background thinking* while they do *certain types* of driving. It can definitely be done if sitting in standstill or slow-moving traffic.]

Yes, time that can be devoted to *background thinking* is also time that can be gainfully used for *virtualization* or *personal thinking*. So, it is up <u>to you</u> to decide and prioritize as to what you want to do – how you want to spend a given block of *quiet time*.

The process involved in *background thinking* is really no different to that of *sleep thinking*. You go through the same steps of formulating the 'issue' and then handing it over to the brain. The difference being that you do not then proceed to fall asleep (other than possibly to take a few cat naps). As with *sleep thinking* you should give your brain a fair number of time (ideally hours) to work on the problem. But, this time does not have to be in one single block. It can be divided across multiple blocks – when you have the right *quiet time*. With practice you brain will get better at 'book marking' your progress so that you can smoothly resume your thought processes later. That is another difference vis-à-vis *sleep thinking*. With *sleep thinking*, as far as you are concerned (though it may not actually be the case within your brain), all of the thinking gets done in 'one block' as you sleep.

Another difference is that there is no wake-up scenario and as such a set time at which to ask your brain for the 'output'. You will have to decide when you want to start asking the brain if there is any meaningful results to be had. You will know. Though it is being done in the *background* you would be aware of what is transpiring. It is all taking place in your brain. So, you will know. You will feel it. You just need to be more aware – and that will happen with the *'brain meditation'*.

There is really no point spending more time on this technique. I have told you all you need to know. I know that you can take it from here. It is not a complicated notion. You just need to work on it – in due course, if you so wish. Start with *sleep thinking*. If that worked well <u>for you</u>, then, down the road, think about *background thinking*.

'Parallel Thinking'
Parallel thinking is hard! Quite a few of you may decide that it is too complicated or that it is not worth the effort. That is fine. A-OK. It is definitely optional and it is definitely not for everyone – the <u>only</u> such technique in this book. It is a value-add for those that feel that they can aspire to this level of brain-specific proactive multitasking.

Parallel thinking is not really a compressed, shorter-timescale version of *background thinking*.

Parallel thinking is about trying to successfully juggle two or more thought-processes, ideally related, at the same time. In general, however, working on **two** related issues at once is plenty sufficient for most. It, like *accelerated thinking*, is meant to be used in short bursts.

With *parallel thinking* the brain will rotate, sequentially, through the issues it has been asked to process. Each issue will alternate between being processed in the foreground to being consigned, temporarily, to lower-priority *background* processing. You will be aware (vaguely be it) of the parallel thought processes taking place. One issue getting prominence at the expense of another.

As with *sleep thinking* and *background thinking* the key to *parallel thinking* is being able to clearly formulate the two (or more) issues you want your brain to tackle. You need them as separate 'thought capsules'. Then you need to have one of those internal, very frank, *within the brain*, talks with your brain. You, in your mind's eye, set the scene for the brain.

Explain, clearly, to your brain what you are trying to achieve. If the two issues are related point out the relationship(s). Draw a mental image of the relationships. Then you ask the brain to please go to work – when it can.

For *parallel thinking* to be most effective you need to be on-the-ball, i.e., focused and concentrating. You need to be alert, driven and receptive. You need to be very much attune and one with your brain. If not, you will not be giving your brain a fair chance. You will miss some of the thought processes that the brain is trying to share with you *on the fly*. Hence, why this is only really possible when you have truly mastered 'brain meditation' and genuinely have a oneness with your brain.

Summary: Power Thinking

CB *'Brain meditation'* conditions you/your brain to make *power thinking* a reality.

CB 'Brain meditation' fine-tunes your brain; it **does not** increase your innate IQ.

CB All three *power thinking* techniques, i.e., **1/** accelerated thinking, **2/** background thinking & **3/** parallel thinking are optional.

CB *Accelerated thinking* is a burst of peak/near peak brain performance – when there is a real **need**.

CB *Accelerated thinking* is *fight or flight* for the brain that <u>does involve</u> **brain chemicals** and electrical charges.

CB A trigger word/phrase is used to invoke *accelerated thinking*.

CB No guarantee that *accelerated thinking* will always satisfy expectations – since it can only work with 'data' it already has or can access.

CB *Background thinking* and *sleep thinking* are very similar.

CB If you master *sleep thinking* you really should try *background thinking* – given the commonalities.

CB You need to give your brain adequate 'quiet time' to complete *background thinking*.

CB You can do *background thinking* while walking, taking a bath, exercising, waiting, eating, travelling, etc.

CB Yes, time that can be allocated for *background thinking* also happens to be time that can be gainfully used for *virtualization* or *thinking for pleasure*.

CB *Parallel thinking* is definitely not for everyone.

CB *Parallel thinking* involves your brain alternating between processing two or more 'issues', one getting more attention at a given time.

ᗡ Only consider *parallel thinking* once you feel that you have graduated 'brain meditation', *cum laude*, and have a true oneness with your (amazing) brain.

Acadia National Park, Maine

Keywords & Phrases From 'Power Thinking'

✓   Conditioning/fine-tuning your brain.

✓   *Intimacy & intensity* of your relationship with your brain.

✓   Accelerated thinking is real; not pie-in-the-sky.

✓   Accelerated thinking = 'up shift', on demand, surge in brain activity.

✓   *Think Faster.*

✓   Brain chemicals kicking in.

✓   Making your brain sprint.

✓   *Fight or flight* for the brain.

✓   No crying wolf.

✓   Brain chemicals.

✓   Sleep thinking/background thinking = two sides of the same coin.

✓   Foreground thinking.

✓   Blocks of 'quiet time'.

✓   Formulating the 'issue'.

✓   Handing the 'issue' over to your brain.

✓   *Parallel thinking* is hard – but is *optional.*

✓   Alert, driven and receptive.

✓   Genuine oneness with your brain.

✓   Think harder.

✓   **Think, think, think.**

✓   Let's go …

7.
PROCESS, SCHEDULE
& EXPECTATIONS

'Brain meditation' is **not** meant to be a casual, short-term dalliance. Instead, it has to be a *long-term, deep-seated* **commitment**, practiced daily. It is, flat-out, a self-help program for changing your life -- for the better. You can't expect to achieve 'life change' without putting in some real effort. 'Brain meditation', as such, does require you to make *crucial changes, henceforth*, in how you go about your day-to-day life. For a start, as you now know, you have to do the virtualizations and the befriending. It is not an arduous program, but you still have to *'pay your dues'*.

'Brain meditation' is **not** meant to provide immediate results. Neither will it. So, please do not expect *'life change'* overnight or within the first week. It will not happen.

The only changes you will notice at first are but small, fleeting, *feel good* blips. These will be due to temporary surges in brain chemicals (such as dopamine) associated with brain interactions such as *virtualization* or *thinking for pleasure*.

Lasting, long-term results, in particular finding **equanimity** (and eventually a deep sense of **serenity**), are achieved cumulatively. They will not be felt for *many months (if not longer)*. And that is provided you *conscientiously* adhere to the program, i.e., good morning ritual, virtualization, mindful thinking, etc., on a *daily basis* (with but an occasional lapse).

You have to always bear in mind that this is a change in lifestyle program. In order for you to get the results you seek you need to *change* your lifestyle. You need to *integrate* 'brain meditation' to be a routine part of your *daily life*. You know the *mantra* by now. Do 'it': *as you brush your teeth, take a shower, stop for a cup of coffee, do some exercise, etc., etc.* {SMILE}

For 'brain meditation' to be effective you can't just do it on a whim, when you feel like it or when you suddenly remember. You cannot continually go on and off the program. It is something that you have to *commit to* and *stick to*. Otherwise you will not get the full benefits. As such it is similar to a diet.

You have to get into the **routine** of doing 'brain meditation' on a **daily basis**.

It will typically take *three to four months* for the 'brain meditation' *routines* to become ingrained into your life. During this initial *imprinting* period it is real important that you do not miss any days of 'brain meditating'. *Skipping a day or two during <u>this acclimatization</u> can set you back.*

Following the *imprinting* period missing a day or two will not be too drastic. However, following the *imprinting* you will invariably be aware of your need to 'brain meditate'. As such it is unlikely that you will have too many 'off' days. Your brain will, with luck, gently remind you that you need to get back on the program.

It is a slow process. <u>But the changes will occur (in time)</u>. Be patient.

> ➢ **'Brain meditation' is such that the changes are inevitable!** ◄

The changes have to happen because you have changed your life to make them happen.

This is not an arduous program. You do not have to devote any dedicated time to it. You do it in timeshare mode – on-the-fly as you get on with your daily life.

There will also be a **lag time** before you notice **changes** that have **already** taken place in your life.

It would not be unusual for you to go for months *without realizing* that 'brain meditation' has changed you. That 'brain meditation' has already started to work. That it has already kicked-in. This (alas) is the ***lag time***; the period of months <u>before you appreciate</u> that certain changes have *already* occurred sometime back.

Though not compulsory it might be easier to first start with the four (4) '*befriending*' routines and work on them for a few weeks before moving onto do virtualization and mindful thinking. But, **SMILE** as much as you can, as often as you can, throughout. {SMILE}

Keywords & Phrases From 'Process, Schedule & Expectations'

✓ **Lifestyle change.**

✓ Immediate results are just the *'feel good'* blips.

✓ Cumulative … long-term … *program*.

✓ *Routine … daily basis.*

✓ Imprinting/Acclimatization period.

✓ *Many months.*

✓ *Changes are inevitable.*

✓ *Not arduous.*

✓ *Lag time* before you realize …

✓ Integrate … ingrained.

✓ Conscientiously adhere to program.

✓ Timeshare mode …. on-the-fly.

✓ Do not skip at the start.

✓ OK, to miss a couple of days after acclimatization.

✓ OK to *befriend* first.

✓ Be patient.

✓ Brain will {*smile*} remind you.

✓ *A process … a regimen.*

✓ Smile, often.

8.
RESULTS, REWARDS
& RISKS

'Brain meditation', in time, will *change you*, for the better. That is a given. The changes are *inevitable* provided you adhere to the program.

Within a few months of embarking on the program you will slowly notice (factoring in the *lag time*) that you are beginning to feel much better about life in general, yourself in particular.

You will start feeling much more *in control* of your life.

You will feel better empowered to *cope* with life's inevitable trials and tribulations.

You will slowly experience a sense of ***peace*** within yourself. In time this will lead to a sense of ***serenity***.

'Brain meditation' will **not** cause you any real harm. It will definitely not lead to or exacerbate any mental illnesses (or conditions). It cannot! There is nothing drastic, dramatic, untoward, devious, underhand, duplicitous, obnoxious or 'naughty' involved. 'Brain meditation' is based entirely on *mindful thinking* and *smiling*. Neither of those can get you into too much trouble (though you might, sometimes, have to be a tad mindful as to who you smile at). {SMILE}

'Brain meditation' does attempt to increase your inborn IQ. That is ***not*** one of its goals. What it is committed to doing, however, is help you *better utilize* the IQ you *already possess*. Making you try and use your brain at close to its full capacity. In will *fine-tune* the IQ you were born with. It will make your brain sharper and more acute. You will be able to feel it – that your brain is more responsive in all situations.

The Rewards Of Brain Meditation

The rewards of 'brain meditation' are all in terms of positive **changes** to **your life**.

These *changes* that you will experience can be divided into **three** categories:

1. Changes in **your demeanor**.

2. Changes in the way **you think**.

3. Changes in the way **you sleep**.

All these changes should (in the main) be self-explanatory, easy to understand, fairly logical, and straightforward to rationalize. As such, this book, given its goal of being a *'quick guide'*, will only touch upon them *briefly*. If you want <u>more detail</u> you will find that in the companion book *"Brain Meditation – For True Productivity and Serenity"*.

Changes In Your Demeanor

These are the changes that many will <u>most look forward</u> to in return for practicing 'brain meditation'.

Five changes that you should expect to see are:

1. Increasing sense of *self-reliance* (and self-confidence).

2. Finding it easier to make *lifestyle changes* (e.g., dieting, exercising, etc.) and being able to <u>stick with them</u>.

3. Learning to *modulate and moderate pain* (with the realization that all pain is perceived in the brain).

4. Acquiring an inner core of *serenity* (following a period of progressive *calmness* within).

5. Realization that you can *see better in the dark*!

Becoming more self-reliant is inevitable – *provided* you want to be as such. Regular virtualization and mindful thinking will make you more self-aware, better prepared, calmer, more alert and less flappable. You might even reach a point where *sanguine* and *phlegmatic* become applicable words when it comes to you. With luck people might comment that: *'if you were more laid back you would run the risk of toppling over'*! This is all good. You will come to enjoy being as such. It is cool. {SMILE}

Over time you will realize that you have become more competent at dealing with life. You will feel a sense of **competency**. You will begin a process of coming to *peace with yourself*. You will eventually **gain** that peace, along with a deep sense of inner *serenity*. There are synergies involved too. And this is how you end-up becoming more self-reliant, more self-confident and achieve that serenity. [Also check the *next chapter*.]

The oneness with your brain fostered through the *befriending* process will make you feel that you '*never walk alone*'.

The *willingness* between you and your *befriended* brain to work together is what makes it easier to realize and maintain lifestyle changes.

Pain: Pain is something that you experience <u>within</u> your brain – though you rarely think of it as such. Pain *per se* is a sensation <u>within</u> your brain. If you are not aware of this *pain-brain* connection it is an intriguing subject that you should look into. Pain (the equivalent of the body's 'check engine' light) is something that most have to contend with. Start by Googling '*pain brain*' or '*all pain is in the brain*'.

[There are some people that are totally immune to pain. They do not feel any pain irrespective of what happens to their bodies. It is, however, not as great as it sounds. These people have to be ultra-careful because they have no way of knowing when damage is being done to their body! A lit match could be burning their finger, but they would be unaware of it.]

First come to terms with the *pain-brain* connection. Then you will see how this program, *laser-focused* on improving your relationship with your brain, will help in trying to manage pain.

Being able to see better in the **dark** has nothing to do with improving your *eyesight* -- within your eyes. It has all to do with your brain being able to *better process* the information it is <u>receiving</u> from your eyes. It is a specialized form of *accelerated thinking*. Your brain extracting more data from the information stream coming from your eyes. Think of it in terms of your *befriended* brain being able to *amplify* the information coming from your eyes so you can, in your brain, see more detail.

Changes In The Way You think

There are eight possible changes that fall into this category. The first three of these already having been dealt with in *earlier chapters*:

1. Ability to problem solve and deliberate on decision making options in your sleep, i.e., *sleep thinking*.

2. Ability, when required, to *shift gears* in the intensity and incisiveness of your thinking, i.e., *accelerated thinking*.

3. Possibility of being able to productively think certain things through in *background mode*, i.e., *background thinking*.

4. Discovering that your brain is providing you with more detailed (and practical) *get out of jail* options when you find yourself in *fight or flight* situations, i.e., <u>subconscious</u> *accelerated thinking* when you are in a bind (e.g., unexpected mishap while driving or a physical threat while out walking).

5. Discovering that you, in general, appear to have *more time* to think things through and get things done; i.e., *faster* and more in-depth processing by your brain resulting in you having *MORE time* to do things (in essence by slowing down your perception of time).

6. Improvement in your ability to *concentrate* and *stay focused* (thanks to the *befriending* protocols and the overall conditioning of your brain due to virtualization and mindful thinking).

7. Discovering that (thanks to *virtualization*, *mindful thinking* and *sleep thinking*) you have become more *decisive*, find it easier to commit to *decisions* you make, and cope better with the consequences of the decisions you make.

8. Discovering that (due to the *oneness* with your brain and *virtualization*) you do not become *exasperated* as often or as fast (as you were prone to in the past).

Changes In The Way You Sleep

There are three potential changes that you should be on the lookout for:

1. Discovering, a few months after the initial *befriending* process, that your *sleep habits* (and patterns) have started to change, for the better – and as such that you are able to sleep more restfully than before.

2. A gradual appreciation that your dreams have become more *pleasant* (and interesting), with a marked decrease in those that would be deemed 'nightmarish'.

3. A realization that your dreams, in addition to being 'pleasanter', have also become more *structured* and *narrative* – i.e., becoming more like watching a good movie or reading an interesting short-story.

It should <u>not</u> be too difficult to rationalize as to how and why these changes are likely to occur. Much, of course, has to do with the overall sense of calmness and the *peace with brain/yourself* that comes with this program. *Befriending*, a key part of this program, definitely is a factor. That the nightly *good night* ritual, ideally with the optional *highlight reel* discipline, plays a role should be obvious.

The Risks Of Brain Meditation

There is really nothing dangerous, bad, insidious, naughty or untoward that one can associate or attribute to 'brain meditation'. There are no drugs, vitamins, supplements, whatsoever, involved. There is nothing additional, beyond this book, that you have to buy. There is no specific physical effort or maneuvers (e.g., having to sit crossed-legged) involved. You don't even have to devote any dedicated time to it.

'Brain meditation', cut to the chase, is all about *mindful thinking*. Furthermore, what you opt to think about is 100% in your control. It is very much a 'YOU, YOU, YOU' program. With *virtualization* you think about YOUR future. It is difficult, if not impossible, to really find fault in this. Consequently, there really is very little risk that you need to worry about.

Five potential risks that you could come up with would be:

1. Others may *not like/trust* the new *thinking you* – in that you have changed (for the better) and some would contend that you have, as such, become 'less fun'.

2. Others may find the new *thinking you* somewhat *intimidating* (albeit for good reason) – i.e., you run the risk of being kept at arms-length as a newly become *nerd*, a *geek*, an *intellectual,* etc.

3. Some may start to consider you as *arrogant*, conceited, condescending, smug, *self-absorbed*, etc., as a way of trying to deal with you having become more *self-confident*, more *self-reliant*, more *decisive* and more *thoughtful*.

4. Given that you can do '*more in less time*' (having to do with the '*slowing down of time*' (mentioned above)) some (stuck in their own slower frame of time), may find you, <u>per their standards</u>, somewhat fast-paced, *reckless*, rash and impetuous.

5. You may (as a result of *virtualization* and *mindful thinking*) start to *overthink* issues. That could lead to a tendency towards being too cautious – i.e., becoming risk averse. As a saying goes you might become a person who

has trouble crossing a log bridge because you can foresee all the potential dangers and mishaps. *Temper this with '4.' above!*

The good news here is that the ***thinking you*** will have the brainpower (i.e., the 'smarts') to be aware of these risks! As such, none of these should catch you off-guard. You have the ability to determine how far you want to proceed with any of these five risks. The new ***thinking you*** will have the requisite smarts to determine if you want to modulate and moderate any of the above listed *detrimental* traits. You will always be in control. So, if you fear that appearing 'arrogant' might become an issue, you will (by then) possess the insights to work out how you could minimize that trait.

The ***thinking you*** will have so much more control over all of you. So, you do not have to become a victim of your new found 'worth'. You have the power and the insights to modulate how you come across. It might not be 100% successful, but you should be able to aim for at least a 70% satisfaction rate.

Two optional virtualization exercises

This self-help book is nearly done. You have been told everything you need to know – including the risks and rewards. It is now up to YOU to put it all into practice. To that end, these two optional virtualization exercises could be beneficial.

1. **1st Virtualization Exercise**: Now that we have touched upon the potential results, rewards and risks, try and imagine yourself as the future *brain befriended, Thinking YOU*. We have talked about the changes you should expect. Now do a bit of constructive daydreaming. Try and *virtualize* the future you. Try and see what it would be like to walk in those new shoes. Role play. Imagine others looking at you, observing you. Go for it. It is all in your mind. Enjoy.

2. **2nd Virtualization Exercise**: This one will be a bit harder than the first. We have talked about *oneness, peace-with-self, calmness* and even that sense of *serenity*. But, if you are yet to start this program these are mere words … aspirations. However, we can *virtualize*. We can daydream the future. Try and see if you can *virtualize* yourself, a few years hence, when your life will be <u>more serene</u>. Think of what this program intends to provide. Extrapolate <u>that</u> to *virtualize* a calmer less stressed life. *Imagine. Virtualize. Hope.* It is all in your mind. {SMILE}

Keywords & Phrases From 'Results, Rewards & Risks'

✓ *Changing you, for the better.*

✓ Nothing dangerous, bad or naughty.

✓ Changes, predominantly positive, are inevitable.

✓ Power to modulate and moderate **pain**.

✓ Sense of *peace* leading to a sense of *serenity*.

✓ *Better empowered to cope.*

✓ No real harm.

✓ More in control of life.

✓ Self-reliance/self-confidence.

✓ See better in the dark!

✓ 'Sanguine' and 'phlegmatic'.

✓ *Willingness* to make lifestyle changes easier.

✓ More decisive.

✓ Less exasperated.

✓ Story-like dreams.

✓ Not liked/not trusted.

✓ Intimidating, arrogant, self-absorbed.

✓ Slowing down perception of time.

✓ *'Get out of jail'* options.

✓ Danger of 'overthinking'.

✓ More time.

✓ *'Never walk alone'.*

9.
THE THINKING
YOU

'Brain meditation', slowly be it, will in time transform you into a *thoughtful* person. *Thoughtful* in this sense would embrace and include:

* *exhibiting careful thought,*

* *predisposed to thought,*

* *consideration to others*, as well as

* *being mindful.*

These, by any standard or measure, are not bad traits to possess. I think you will be happy being a *thoughtful* person. That you will become as such should not come as a surprise. 'Brain meditation' as you must have realized by now revolves around being *thoughtful.*

Within this context of being *thoughtful* some of the other words that might apply to the future 'thinking you' could be: *reflective … considerate … heedful … contemplative* and *mindful.*

These are all good words. Great attributes. Attributes to be proud of, attributes worth aspiring to. Reflect on that. Being *reflective* can be real cool.

The word, however, that will *best* describe the future 'brain meditating' you is **cerebral** – i.e., *of or relating to the brain.* There is nothing pejorative about being *cerebral.* Anybody who has issues with you being *cerebral* is suffering from a major case of 'sour grapes'! Cut to the chase, being *cerebral* is what you are striving towards – i.e., achieving oneness with your brain. So, please don't let the word *cerebral* stand in the way. Embrace it. Savor it. *Visualize the future <u>cerebral you</u>.* See how tall and proud YOU stand. The cerebral, self-reliant you.

THE MASTER OF YOUR UNIVERSE, THE MASTER OF YOUR DESTINY.

The cerebral you that will never walk alone.

You will invariably be very much in accord with your surroundings and those that are around you. You will be more *attuned* with where you are, both physically and psychologically. You will become increasingly more *perspicacious*, i.e., discerning and insightful. You will see more; you will notice more. It all has to do with your enhanced *brain power*.

Actually, there will be a bit more to it than that. And that will be the '**extra time**' you will generally enjoy; i.e., your brain working faster and sharper thus giving you an edge when it comes to time. [It is real cool.]

You should inevitably, in any situation/scenario, be half-a-step ahead (if not more) of where you would have been ***prior to*** 'brain meditation'. This is the 'extra time' phenomenon.

A few years into 'brain meditation' you will slowly start to realize you are less rushed, more relaxed, more laid-back. Not much will faze you, anymore. *Equanimity will be a constant companion.*

Not only will you not walk alone, you will always walk with much more composure.

In a crisis you will be ***calmer*** than most. While others flail, you will be very focused, and to an extent emotionless while your brain races ahead determining what needs to be done next. In crisis situations, more often than not, you will emerge as a leader (as opposed to a follower).

You, in a crisis, will be a ***trained and proficient thinker*** -- capable of working out alternatives quicker and with more clarity than others. Plus, you will always have that '***extra time***'. You will, in addition, be ***icy cold*** inside – intent on finding solutions rather than reacting to what has already happened. <u>Unflappable</u>.

The world around you will become more vivid and vibrant. *You will see and experience the world in High Definition (HD)!*

You will see the world in a different light – a light that is more intense and probing.

You will acquire a renewed *fascination* with all that which surrounds you. There will be an enhanced sense of *wonder, awe and fascination.*

You will see more of the world around you than you did before.

You will become even more inquisitive. You will want to experience and savor everything – much more, and more acutely.

Life will feel richer, fuller and more rewarding.

You will appreciate life and what you have in a more profound sense.

Life will seem easier to live -- and to contend with.

You will feel so much more alive!

Empowered ... and feeling *privileged* to be you, the **Thinking You**.

<u>All of this</u> because your brain will now be processing more data (faster and in more depth) than ever before. It is akin to getting a new, faster computer – though in your case what you have done is *tune*, energize and declutter the one you always had 'up there'. Your *befriended brain* is now processing the input from all your senses to a higher degree of 'clarity'. *Hence, the HD!*

You will be more organized, competent and dependable.

Yes, there is a danger that you will encounter some resentment and jealousy. People will notice that your life is different. That your life appears to be 'fuller', more vibrant, and more often than not on a calm, 'even keel'. This potential resentment/jealousy, alas, is a risk/price you have to contend with, weighed against the manifold benefits you will gain from 'brain meditation'. But, life always will remain a *compromise*. You, however, are now better equipped than ever before to effectively deal with such compromises. So, make the decision as to how you want to proceed. An empowered *Thinking You* with all the benefits (per this program), or just continuing as your current self?

Thinking will define you.

There is a French saying from the 18th century: *"People are governed by the head; a kind heart is of little value in chess".*

You will not let yourself become a cold, dull, calculating, automaton. Your befriended brain will not let you be as such. Instead, you will be interesting, you will be alive, you will be energized.

AND a sense of **_serenity_** will enter your life. Years from now it will be both the *Thinking You* and the *Serene You*.

It is now up to you to start this program, in earnest. Start practicing 'brain meditation' on a daily basis, sans compromise. It is time to stop all procrastination and take the first steps towards becoming the new **_Thinking You_**.

Keywords & Phrases From 'The Thinking YOU'

✓ *Cerebral.*

✓ *Thoughtful … mindful … reflective … contemplative … considerate.*

✓ Perspicacious.

✓ Attuned – physically & psychologically.

✓ **Much more alive!**

✓ *Empowered … privileged.*

✓ Life seen in HD.

✓ Equanimity will be a constant companion.

✓ Extra Time!

✓ <u>Unflappable</u>.

✓ Trained & proficient thinker.

✓ *Never walk alone.*

✓ Calm → → *icy cold.*

✓ Empowered.

✓ Richer, fuller & more rewarding.

✓ *Faster/in-depth processing of input from senses.*

✓ Better at compromise than ever before.

✓ **Risk**: resentment & jealousy.

✓ *Easier to live … easier to contend with.*

✓ Sense of serenity.

✓ Thinking will define you.

✓ *Feel much more alive!*

Happy Thinking.

Let me share with you, in friendship and support,
my motto in life:
"Think Free, Or Die".

Bon Chance,
and may your brain always be
one with you.

☺ ☺ FINI ☺ ☺

Partial Index

Accelerated thinking   48 – 51, 53 – 54, 56, 62 - 63

Background mode   1, 24, 30, 63

Background thinking   48 - 49, 51 – 54, 56, 63

Befriending brain   1 – 2, 7, 11, 13 – 19, 21, 23, 25, 32, 34, 41, 57 – 59, 62 – 65, 69 – 70

Brushing teeth   1, 6, 17, 24, 26 – 28, 34

Buddhism   6

Chemicals, brain ...1, 3, 9, 12, 17, 21, 25, 29, 49 – 51, 54, 56 - 57

Concentration   53

Daydream   25, 31, 36, 65

Dopamine   1, 3, 9, 12 – 13, 17, 21, 23, 25, 57

Dreams...16, 21, 25, 39, 43 – 44, 63, 65 - 66

Exasperation   63, 66

Exercise   1, 6, 9, 11, 17 -18, 22, 25, 31 - 33, 35, 57, 65

Focus   1 – 3, 5 – 9, 11 – 13, 26 – 27, 29, 31 – 32, 34, 36, 53, 62 – 63, 68

'Good morning' ritual   14 – 15, 17, 21 – 23, 33, 50, 57

'Good night' ritual   14 – 17, 21, 33, 42 – 44, 50, 57, 63 - 64

HInduIsm   6

Keywords   13, 23, 36, 47, 56, 59, 66, 71

Meditation   1 – 13, 16 – 20, 22, 24 – 27, 29, 31 – 38, 40 – 42, 45, 48 – 49, 51 – 55, 57 – 58, 60 – 61, 64, 67 – 69

Pain   41, 61 – 62, 66

Parallel Thinking   44, 48 – 49, 52 - 56

Personal Thinking   38 – 39, 41, 45, 47, 52

Religion   5 – 6, 11, 13, 39

Rewards   9, 32 -33, 42, 60 – 61, 63, 65 - 66

Risks   2, 9, 60 - 66

Sleep thinking   42 – 49, 51 – 54, 56, 62 - 63

Summaries   11, 21, 34, 45, 54

Timeshare mode   6, 8, 11, 13, 24, 26 – 27, 29 – 30, 33 – 34, 58 - 59

Thinking
    Accelerated   see 'Accelerated thinking'
    Background   see 'Background thinking'
    Parallel   see 'Parallel thinking'
    Personal   see 'Personal thinking'
    Sleep   see 'Sleep thinking'

Virtualization   1 – 2, 6 – 7, 9 – 11, 13, 25 – 36, 38 – 41, 45, 52, 54, 57 -58, 61, 63 - 65

Visualization   6, 11, 13, 25 – 26, 34, 36

Yoga   5, 9, 11, 17, 25

www.ingramcontent.com/pod-product-compliance
Lightning Source LLC
Chambersburg PA
CBHW081205180526
45170CB00006B/2217